The Unstoppable Sales Machine

The Unstoppable Sales Machine

How to Connect, Convert, and Close New Customers

Shawn Casemore

Routledge
Taylor & Francis Group

A PRODUCTIVITY PRESS BOOK

First published 2023
by Routledge
605 Third Avenue, New York, NY 10158

and by Routledge
4 Park Square, Milton Park, Abingdon, Oxon, OX14 4RN

Routledge is an imprint of the Taylor & Francis Group, an informa business

ISBN: 978-1-032-18056-4 (hbk)
ISBN: 978-1-032-18054-0 (pbk)
ISBN: 978-1-003-25264-1 (ebk)

DOI: 10.4324/9781003252641

Typeset in Minion
by Apex CoVantage, LLC

This book is dedicated to the hundreds of clients I've had the good fortune to work with since I first launched my speaking and consulting business in 2009. Your confidence, trust, and willingness to try new things has been both inspiring and rewarding.

Contents

Foreword

Saul of Tarsus, born sometime after the birth of Christ, would have been in his early twenties when Christ was engaged in his ministry. Originally virulently anti-Christian, he had his epiphany on the Road to Damascus and became the second most important person in the Christian Church, and eventually, became known as St. Paul.

He was also the first viral marketer.

Paul the Apostle would preach the gospel in Corinth, Antioch, Rome, Jerusalem, and other places, and would urge his listeners to each go tell others. Christianity grew to 30 million followers by the year 350 out of a total population of about 190 million globally, having begun with just 12 adherents three and a half centuries prior. The statisticians and demographers find that growth stunning.

But that growth was "unstoppable" in that people were eager to spread the good news, and did so without the aid of any kind of mass communication at all, other than the human voice in one's presence.

Twenty-five years ago, circa 1998, there were no smartphones, Google, podcasts, Wikipedia, Netflix, Swiffer, Airbnb, GPS, Uber, Blockchain; and these organizations that did exist, exist no more: Ringling Brothers, Pier 1, Borders, A&P, Toys"R"Us, Compaq, Henri Bendel, and Blockbuster.

Initiatives, companies, causes, and what seem like "evergreen" organizations are simply not permanent. However, some have managed far longer life cycles and evolutions than others. They *can* become, with the help of brilliant leadership and constant innovation, "unstoppable."

Shawn Casemore has focused on this type of "perpetual motion machine" in terms of sales and growth. He examines the competition, the changing nature of buyers, how to build and sustain the "machine," and the inevitable turbulence that must be anticipated and exploited—and I'm writing this in a post-pandemic world filled with what I've termed "new realities."

His Unstoppable Sales Machine is more important than ever in this time of "no-normal."™ Learn here how to identify, pursue, and convince your ideal buyers of your value and worth. Master the techniques that are essential to achieve market dominance, no matter what market you're in, no matter what your size.

With modern techniques and cogent strategies, Shawn takes you through the myths and minefields of sales strategies and tactics and demonstrates how great companies become irresistible forces that can, indeed, overcome immovable objects. After all, the world today has over six billion people, and they're all potential customers for someone.

Perhaps this book and these approaches can be your epiphany. You don't need to travel to Corinth or Antioch; you simply need to sit with this book and, perhaps, reach for your computer. You can influence the world, and you can provide value to customers that creates unstoppable growth.

I urge you to do that, and to be as successful as Paul. After all, isn't one-sixth of the world an attractive growth goal?

—Alan Weiss, PhD
Alan Weiss is the author of over 60 books
appearing in 15 languages. *Million Dollar Consulting*
(McGraw-Hill) has been on the
shelves for 30 years and is in its sixth edition.
His latest book, with Lisa Larter, is
Masterful Marketing (Bloomsbury Press).

Preface

This book is written for business owners, sales executives, leaders, and professionals—anyone who has the desire to create a rapid and sustained increase in their sales, without having to invest a significant amount of time or money in doing so.

It's a comprehensive review of my work with clients from around the globe, introducing what I call Unstoppable Selling. Building on my work with Unstoppable Organizations, this book captures the strategies and tactics my clients have used that allow them predictability in their sales, while letting them sleep more soundly at night.

To ensure you have the most current and up-to-date information, there will be a virtual appendix available immediately at www.unstoppable salesmachine.com. You can visit this site anytime at no cost to obtain my latest models and thinking relative to building your very own Unstoppable Sales Machine.

My latest thinking, models, tools, and resources are contained here, including the Unstoppable Sales Strategic Multiplier, Hybrid Sales Funnel, Velocity Stack, and Customer Empowerment Model. I'll also be demonstrating how you can quickly establish your *Unstoppable Sales Machine* regardless of the size of your company, or the sector you're in. If you sell business to business, then the *Unstoppable Sales Machine* will work for you, like it's worked for countless others.

Finally, introducing your machine will not require you to hire a bunch of experts or more employees. In fact, many of my clients have been able to redeploy their current staff as your machine can automate much of the activities that will be required if you so choose. This is a book that accepts you where you are, and then walks you through the steps to quickly introduce and launch your very own Unstoppable Sales Machine. You'll find all the advice, guidance, case studies, and worksheets contained in this one convenient book, ready for you to implement.

If you intend to scale your sales, or you simply want more freedom from the day-to-day roller coaster of your current sales, then this is the book for you.

I've written this book because sales is a noble profession. It is at the heart and soul of every company, yet the continued evolution of today's customers and how they engage with, select, and buy products and services requires that we rethink how we approach selling. I'll show you how to become an expert at selling, while having the freedom and comfort in knowing that your machine will never let you down.

Shawn Casemore
Chatsworth, Ontario, CA
January 2022

Acknowledgments

First off, I owe a great deal of gratitude to Alan Weiss, the author of over 60 books in 15 languages and the thought leader in solo consulting. Alan's coaching, guidance, and feedback helped me learn how to sell myself (even when I didn't believe it was possible), and more importantly, helped me change my mindset relative to what is possible. I am forever grateful.

My wife Julie has always been supportive in everything I do, even if she doesn't fully understand why I do it. I'll never forget the day I walked into our kitchen while she was off work pregnant with our firstborn and told her I was quitting my job to start my own business in consulting. She barely flinched.

My thanks to Michael Sinocchi, Publisher at Taylor and Francis. Without his support, this book wouldn't exist.

Lastly, a heartfelt thank-you to all my clients for your continued belief in me, my work, and your willingness to try new things. The results we've achieved are a testament to your dedication to success.

About the Author

Shawn Casemore began selling at the age of 11, knocking on doors in his neighborhood to sell his services for cutting lawns and painting fences. Today Shawn helps companies all around the world introduce what he calls Unstoppable Selling™.

As a consultant, speaker, advisor, and author, Shawn has traveled the globe working with organizations such as PepsiCo, Tim Hortons, and BMO bank to name a few. He speaks regularly at conferences and private events on topics related to accelerating sales in today's new economy.

Shawn lives in Ontario, Canada with his family and you can visit him online at ShawnCasemore.com.

Introduction

March 14, 2020, was the day that marked one of the most significant shifts in sales of my career. Sure, I can recall other dates, like the date I started my first job in sales. On March 14, however, our family vacation in Davenport, Florida, was interrupted by sudden shutdowns, business closures, and general panic among the public.

The date's significance marks the sudden rise in popularity of what many refer to as "virtual selling." Unable to visit buyers in person, sales professionals across the country and the globe suddenly reverted to using Zoom and Microsoft Teams for their sales presentations.

What's most interesting about the emergence of virtual selling is that it wasn't new. Companies and sales professionals have been selling without ever seeing their buyers in person for years.

In the months and years that have followed, what's become readily apparent is that every company that expects to sell needs to build a systematic way of doing so. Gone are the days of hiring a salesperson, setting some targets to achieve (often without having any method to confirm if they can achieve the targets), and then crossing your fingers they'll hit them. Instead, it's similar to betting on a horse race. After studying the statistics of the horses, through a combination of stats and gut feel, you invest in hopes of winning. Sometimes you do, but most times, it's a bust.

It's for this reason I wrote this book. Since that date, the changes we've seen in sales have forever changed selling as a discipline. Today, sales professionals need a more robust toolbox of skills. They need skills extending beyond knowing how to ask questions and influence others. They need to be adept at using technology and working collaboratively with other departments such as marketing and customer service.

DOI: 10.4324/9781003252641-1

To suggest that sales and the discipline of selling have changed then would be an understatement on my part. But we can't just look at our salespeople's skills and think that adding more tools is enough. It isn't. Companies dominating today's marketplace, of which I share dozens of examples, have built a machine of sorts. That's what this book is about, and it's my mission to help you develop your own sales machine, one that is unstoppable.

In Part 1, we'll discuss what has changed in sales and why you need to introduce your very own Unstoppable Sales Machine. Chapter 1 will dive into what an Unstoppable Sales Machine is and why you need one. Then in Chapters 2 and 3, we'll discuss how a sales machine will help you get in front of and sell to today's buyers. Lastly, in Chapter 4, we'll discuss what will happen if you don't act now to build your sales machine.

In Part 2, we'll introduce the various components of your Unstoppable Sales Machine and how to deploy them. In Chapter 5, I'll walk you through the eight components of your sales machine and how to introduce them. Then in Chapters 6 and 7, we'll discuss how to attract and convert today's buyers. Lastly, in Chapters 8 and 9, I'll help you get your entire organization on board with supporting your machine.

Moving into Part 3, we'll discuss how to launch your machine and some pitfalls to avoid. In Chapter 10, I'll discuss some common pitfalls you'll want to be prepared for, then in Chapter 11, I'll share some ways you can accelerate your results. For those eager, we'll discuss how to scale up your sales in Chapter 12, and in the event you need to, how you can scale back your sales as well. Lastly, if you want to crank up your machine, Chapter 13 discusses how you can use your Unstoppable Sales Machine to dominate your market.

YOUR FIRST STEP TO SELLING SUCCESS

This book is a playbook. If you follow the steps as I've laid out, in the order I've laid them out, then you'll have success in introducing your Unstoppable Sales Machine. However, this will require some work. Suggesting you can introduce your very own Unstoppable Sales Machine with just a snap of your fingers would be ludicrous.

If you stay the course and remain committed to launching your machine, you'll increase the level of control you have over your sales. Moreover, doing so will bring you peace of mind and satisfaction that you'll always be able to sell more no matter what future challenges the economy or market might throw at you.

Part 1

New Age Selling
What It Takes to Sell in Today's Evolving Marketplace

Selling is one of the oldest professions, dating back to when we bartered for food and other goods. Despite this, how we sell has evolved immensely, as our buyers and their needs, expectations, and preferences have evolved. Unfortunately, too many companies, executives, and sales leaders still practice sales as if they lived in prehistoric times. We don't, so it's time to find a new method to sell, one that breaks down any preconceived notions of what our buyers want and need if they are to invest in today's market.

DOI: 10.4324/9781003252641-2

1

What Is an Unstoppable Sales Machine (and Why Do I Need One)?

THE FOUR THINGS THAT ARE STOPPING YOUR SALES

There has been a growing divide in how businesses of any size sell their products or services. First, there's what I call the "old-school" method of sales—meeting with people to share gourmet meals, overly expensive coffees, and maybe even a few rounds of golf, eventually convincing them to buy your product or service. Traditionally this is how manufacturers, distributors, professional service firms, managed service providers, and SaaS companies have sold.

Then we have what some might consider a more "modern" approach to sales. Terms like funnels, digital marketing, ad spend, social media, and landing pages scatter across this landscape. The method drives prospective customers from wherever they are to a landing page and then converts them to paying customers from this point. Conversion comes from written copy, an explainer video, or for complex products or services, there may be a call or demonstration.

This approach is increasingly common for companies that sell apps, software, and other products or services delivered online.

Then along comes the pandemic.

Regardless of your approach to selling pre-pandemic, new challenges presented themselves. Companies that used the old-school way of selling could no longer visit with customers with travel stifled. Even companies that sold their products or services online were directly impacted by skyrocketing online advertising costs.

To make matters worse, proven methods to reach prospects and customers that were once effective quickly deteriorated as phone lines went

DOI: 10.4324/9781003252641-3

unanswered, as did emails, which fast accumulated in the wake of the world moving online.

Regardless of how they sold before the pandemic, companies and the executives that led them approached this new challenge predominantly in one of four ways:

1. **A Blockade**: Like a highway being closed, the challenges presented by the pandemic and ensuing shifts in how customers preferred to buy seemed impossible to overcome. The perception was that since their ability to meet with customers and prospects was off the table, their ability to sell was also no longer possible.
2. **Surmountable**: Some companies believed that the challenges presented by the pandemic were surmountable. Like a tree blocking the road. Whether you cut the tree up or drag it off the road, moving forward would require effort, but it was not a complete blockade to their ability to sell.
3. **A Mere Hindrance**: Some companies approached this new world as a mere hindrance, like water blocking a part of the road. They recognized that although some approaches to selling had been directly impacted and possibly changed forever, there were other methods to sell that they could pursue.
4. **Minor Annoyance**: Like a pothole in the road, some companies considered the pandemic as an annoyance. They recognized that by accelerating their testing speed and adopting new sales approaches, they could propel themselves to new sales revenues without ever skipping a beat. Best of all, the faster they could do this, the greater chance they had of capturing market share from their competitors.

These barriers represent the mindset behind sales. Those that viewed the challenges presented by the pandemic as a mere hindrance very quickly adopted new approaches and went on to have record sales revenue. Those who foresaw the limitations provided by the pandemic as impossible are no longer in business.

Case Study: Connecting with Customers during a Pandemic

A client had historically built relationships by having salespeople and sales representatives meet with would-be and existing customers face to face. When the pandemic hit, they initially decided to wait and see what would happen. As with many, there was a belief (or possibly a hope) that they would be able to return to business as usual, meeting with prospects and customers within a few weeks. However, as the weeks turned into months, their sales (and leads) began to fall off, leaving them in a precarious position.

We treated the situation as a minor annoyance, introducing and testing various methods to connect with and reach customers. We used a combination of phone, email, and direct mail to reconnect with existing customers and introduce the company to prospective customers. Information collected during dialogues about customer circumstances by industry was compiled and used to develop scripts and direct mail pieces for prospects in similar industries. Additionally, all outreach commenced focusing on the customer and their situation, asking if there was any way to help versus trying to make a sale.

Within the first eight months of the pandemic, sales returned to previous levels, and new leads and sales steadily increased. Furthermore, my client handled these new activities in-house, which precluded any need to use outside sales reps as travel was limited or restricted entirely; these new approaches to selling reduced the cost of business acquisition, providing a wholly new method of selling.

OLD-SCHOOL "FEET ON THE STREET" SELLING IS DEAD

If you've been making sales predominantly due to having someone visit a customer face to face, you're in trouble. Sure, there will always be some industries in which this form of bonding and connection is still acceptable, but as baby boomers retire and the age of today's buyers becomes younger,[1] their preferences for searching, engaging with, and buying are changing.

A recent study conducted by Marketo[2] found the top ways today's B2B buyers engage with a brand or company are:

1. Visiting their website
2. Email

3. Online communities
4. Chat
5. Social media
6. Mobile device/apps
7. Podcasts/webinars
8. Blogs
9. Video

What's most important from this research is not how today's buyers prefer to engage but what's driving this behavior change. Of course, the pandemic itself only served to accelerate the shift in how prospects and buyers choose to engage with a company or its sales team to research and buy its products or services. But if you peel the onion, you'll notice what's lurking behind the curtain is a shift in the demographic of today's buyers.

During the past several years, my research has identified five specific characteristics of today's younger generation of buyers, all of which serve to inform prospecting, conversion, and closing strategies to sell in today's marketplace.

BUYING PREFERENCES OF TODAY'S YOUNGER GENERATIONS

Search for New Products and Services via the Internet

Younger generations today search for and select products and services using one of three primary methods:

1. They search using Google.
2. They ask their social networks (i.e., Facebook, LinkedIn, Messenger).
3. They consider products or services displayed on social networks.

The latter is only effective for those products or services a customer would expect to find in a social network. As time progresses, the list of what is acceptable versus what is not is expanding as more and more businesses shift their model to include online and virtual services for their customers.

Engage in Online Social Groups to Obtain Input and Referrals

Online platforms like Reddit and Quora have made a business from becoming an online repository for questions and answers. On a smaller scale, LinkedIn groups, Facebook groups, and various online chat groups and forums offer a similar solution, providing buyers a meaningful and convenient way to obtain social input, feedback, and ideas. Sure, buyers might ask their friends for information, but today, younger generations are much more comfortable expanding their reach to a larger and predominantly online social sphere.

Let Online Reviews and Comments Guide Their Decision-Making

Today's generations have become accustomed to seeking input from strangers to inform their decision-making. As a result, reviewing online comments, ratings, and various other online feedback has become a significant influencer of their decisions.

Consider the impact that online platforms like GlassDoor (www.glassdoor.com), an online repository of employee ratings for companies where they've worked, have on employee hiring and retention. Employees today can (and will) review a company online before they ever attend an interview. If reviews from previous employees are wrong, they'll skip the interview (often not even giving notice of their intent).

What's most interesting about this is that today's younger generations will solicit, trust, and accept input from people who participate in a platform with no personal relationship. So, if you've been solely focusing on relationship selling, think again.

Expect a Quick and Simple Buying Experience

If there's one thing *we've all come to expect today*, it's a simple buying experience: no lengthy contracts, no hurdles to jump through. Simple and easy is the key.

This approach to buying is an absolute expectation of today's younger generation of buyers. Why stand in the line at a traditional bank when you can do all your banking online? Why visit a car dealership to buy a car when you can make the entire purchase without ever meeting anyone? One of the reasons online buying has become so popular is that there's no need to speak with anyone. The buying experience is entirely in the hands of the buyer.

If you want to sell to a younger generation of buyers, the process had better be easy to understand and navigate. The simpler, the better. If your "process" is too lengthy or requires a complex contract for review, you're likely never to make a sale to today's younger buyers.

Keep Sales Activities Separate from Social Activities

One of our most exciting findings was the separation of social activities from buying activities. Historically, it was common to take a prospect to lunch or dinner. Over a meal, a business topic would arise, opportunities were discussed, and invariably both parties would strike a deal, often before dessert. Thus, blending social and sales activities were the norm.

Today, younger generations are less inclined to mix business with pleasure. A study by Tork found that 40% of millennials don't even take a lunch break.[3] If combining business with pleasure by taking your buyer to lunch is part of your current sales strategy, you're going to have to find another strategy.

Of course, there are other distinctions, but these five represent the most significant shifts that impact companies that have historically used face-to-face strategies to sell their wares.

Before you run off and start to update your website and build some online landing pages, hold on. I'm not suggesting you need to jump on the bandwagon of introducing hands-off online selling strategies and shoehorn them into your existing sales and business processes. *Instead, it would help if you revisited how your ideal customers or clients prefer finding and selecting your products or services today and in the months and years to come.*

It's time to develop an entirely new system for selling—an Unstoppable Sales Machine of sorts that will drive more qualified leads and result in their conversion to adopt your product or service.

STORIES FROM THE SALES FLOOR

A year ago, one of my clients had been selling their products through reps. They invested heavily in these relationships over the years. Although representatives had brought significant sales 10–15 years ago, they were recently bringing fewer and fewer relationships (and sales) to the table.

Wanting to help my client shift to a more practical approach, I interviewed several of their key customers and several of the sales reps who worked on their accounts. The results weren't surprising yet were decisive in understanding and navigating selling in today's marketplace. First, the demographic of their buyer was changing. The older employees who had purchased from them (and met with sales reps and agents face to face) had or were retiring. Their replacements were considerably younger and more apt to use technology to search for and engage a company. What was the primary method these younger buyers used to search for my client's products? Google.

By investing in an updated website, incorporating various search engine optimization (SEO) strategies, and launching several online methods to connect with website visitors, like chat and WhatsApp, they could connect with these new buyers and begin recovering lost sales. In the first few weeks of launching the chat module alone, they made a half-dozen sales to new customers.

Younger generations today aren't like their predecessors. Yet, we're still using past processes to prospect, convert, and close that were proven nearly 20 years ago, rather than consistently seeking new ways to get in front of and connect with our buyers' changing needs and preferences.

FUNNEL FALSE HOPES: YOU CAN'T SELL EVERYTHING ONLINE

Just because feet-on-the-street selling is dead doesn't mean you throw everything you have into selling online. Unfortunately, this seems to be the perception of some seeking new methods to sell. A recent study by Small Business Trends identified that 62% of businesses fail using Facebook ads.[4]

I should know because I've tried it myself. Being a sales consultant has always been about building trusted relationships, yet I decided in early 2019 to begin testing sales funnels for my business. After spending thousands on running ads on various social media platforms, the results became apparent. Some products and services just can't be sold online. Often the only companies making real money selling solely online are charging you to create and update the ads.

Since then, I've worked with multiple companies who thought building online sales funnels was the answer. Instead, they spent tens of thousands of dollars to attract unqualified leads, with a meager conversion rate and an even lower customer retention rate. Their realization is a message everyone needs to heed. Selling online can be ugly.

I've found that online sales funnels can work well depending on what you are selling, but they are not your only solution to selling. Instead, they offer a channel to sell that engages effectively with your ideal customer or client.

For example, if you are trying to sell widgets to a manufacturer or pipe to a plumber, an online sales funnel will NOT be effective. Alternatively, if you are selling a recipe book or accessories for a mountain bike, you're likely to have much more success. On the other hand, companies like Dollar Shave Club, Shopify, and Netflix use online sales funnels, have tremendous success, and sell to retail customers.

It also bears mentioning that online sales funnels are not a new concept. They are simply a different take on direct marketing, which has been around for hundreds of years. You may have at some point received an envelope in the mail that had some odd colors or fonts, begging you to open it. When you did, there was a long sales letter with various colors, fonts, and underlines. At the end of the letter was an offer you couldn't resist. Online sales funnels are simply a modern marketing approach to direct marketing.

The lesson is quite clear. Not everything can be sold online or using an online sales funnel. However, what can be effective *is to identify the best channels to attract, engage, and convert your customers,* using a combination of both online and offline sources.

Let's look at some common examples of using channels to sell that you've likely participated in recently.

EXAMPLES OF SALES CHANNELS THAT INCORPORATE BOTH ONLINE AND OFFLINE RESOURCES

- You visit a website, enter your mailing information, and receive a free catalog.
- After seeing a retail store, you receive an email that invites you back for a special sale.

- Upon making a purchase online, you receive a discount coupon in the mail for your next order.
- You read an event ad in an online magazine, attend the event, then receive additional information by mail afterward.

When you think about it, we are participating in sales channels all the time. Those effects aren't limited to landing pages and sequenced emails but rather create an experience that connects the prospect with our brand, our promise, and our products or services.

IN AN ONLINE WORLD, RELATIONSHIPS STILL MATTER

Whether you are selling a widget, software, or life insurance, relationships still matter. People only buy from those they know, like, and trust. The key, then, whether we are selling face to face, virtually, or via the telephone, is to use sales channels that help build trust and attract prospects to us. Sending a barrage of cold emails doesn't build trust. Neither does sending an unsolicited text message or making a cold call. Figure 1.1 demonstrates the value of building trust over time.

What these strategies can do, however, is open the door to starting a relationship, but it can be tricky. For example, making a cold call in the

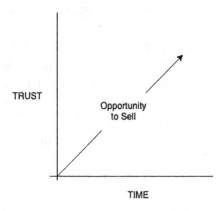

FIGURE 1.1
Time vs. Trust.

wrong manner can instantly turn a prospect off. Likewise, sending an email about you and your product will instantly turn off any prospect.

When it comes to building your Unstoppable Sales Machine, it's about creating a personalized experience for your customers. You can achieve this by using a combination of interactions that allow customers to become aware of your products and services and assess them from a distance before they jump right in.

An early mentor of mine once said, "There are seven billion people in the world. How many will you build a relationship with today?" Powerful. Even in my early days of selling cars, I recall thinking that my market was limited to the surrounding area's population. I believed that, based on the number of past customers, considering our local population, my selling ability was capped. There was no way I could sell enough cars to generate a salary that mimicked what similar salespeople at our sister dealerships did in big cities. I was wrong.

I recall the dealership owner telling us during a sales meeting one day that the top salesman for our brand across the country lived in a small community not far from us. The numbers he sold seemed staggering, and I was confident the story wasn't true. Maybe it wasn't, but later that month, I met a prospective customer that lived two hours away. She had a relative in the area and was out car shopping. While driving by, she stopped in, and after having some discussions and sharing information back and forth, she returned the following weekend to buy a car from me.

In most instances, the owner had told us not to spend much time with any "out-of-town" prospects because they were unlikely to buy from us. Yet, I had made the sale by ignoring that advice and focusing on building a solid relationship.

Herein lies the problem with many of the so-called online sales funnels. They don't ever suggest that a relationship is necessary. It may be that such relationships are unnecessary, but having worked in over a half-dozen industries, I've never found it to be true. My experience includes working in manufacturing, retail, not-for-profit, insurance, financial planning, banking, software, distribution, and wholesale, to name a few. In every instance, sales are tied to relationships because relationships build trust.

You might be wondering exactly how you can build a relationship if you haven't (or aren't) ever going to see your prospect. Unfortunately, there is no short answer to this question, but in my experience, there are eight areas that you must address for any buyer to want to connect and work with you if they can't at least initially get to meet you.

HOW TO BUILD A RELATIONSHIP FROM A DISTANCE

1. Understand your buyers' current circumstances:
   a. What are their priorities?
   b. What challenges do they face?
   c. How can you helpfully add value?
2. Be knowledgeable about their unique challenge(s):
   a. What specific problems do their present difficulties pose for them?
   b. What are other solutions out there to solve their issues?
   c. Why aren't these other solutions effective? If they are, what's missing?
3. Be crystal clear on how your solution (product or service) can help:
   a. What would your prospect find most helpful about your answer?
   b. How does your answer differ from anything else on the market today?
   c. Why is now the right time to use/apply your solution?
4. Be credible in the marketplace:
   a. Can your buyer easily find evidence of how you've helped others?
   b. Can your buyer relate to the others you've helped?
   c. Has your product or service been helping others for a reasonable period?
5. Be transparent:
   a. Is it clear as to who is behind your company (you, your team, etc.)?
   b. Is your offer to your buyer easy to understand?
   c. Is your journey to offering your product or service clear to your customer?
6. Be accessible:
   a. Can your buyers find you easily?
   b. Can your buyers reach you easily?
   c. Do you engage across multiple channels such as email, telephone, and text?

7. Be responsive:
   a. Do you respond to customer inquiries within hours, not days?
   b. Are you following up if the first attempt to reach your buyer goes unanswered?
   c. Is there someone available to answer immediate questions if your buyer needs help?
8. Deliver on your promise(s):
   a. Does your product or service do what you say it will?
   b. Do you provide the support and back up any warranty issues?
   c. Do you respond promptly to inquiries or issues?

Domino's is a longstanding and easy-to-recognize example of these relationship-building steps in practice. Regardless of whether you've heard of Domino's or not, their "delivered in 30 minutes or it's free" is valuable to their buyer, who typically wants warm pizza in a short period. They've been upholding this promise for so long that when you want good pizza delivered in under 30 minutes, Domino's is typically the first choice for many.

Alternatively, when I contact my bank for service, it typically takes at least two days for anyone to respond. Most banks are a great example of how not to build trust. There's often a perception that trust-building using the steps above isn't necessary because we all need a bank after all. My banker typically takes two days to respond to my emails, and I know him! The only reason most of us stay with our current bank is that it's too much work to leave—changing accounts, paying out a mortgage. Banks know this, so they, in my experience, place minimal effort on using any of the eight steps above to build trusting relationships from afar.

You'll notice that by addressing each of the eight points above, not only can you form a relationship before the prospect ever reaches out, but you also, in turn, build trust and rapport before you ever get a chance to speak. These are the foundational principles for your Unstoppable Sales Machine, and they need to be addressed both at a macro (company) level and a micro (individual customer) level.

With these points in mind, let's dig into how we get and keep the attention of today's buyers.

2

Course Correction: How to Get the Attention of Today's Buyers

Today's buyers are more prescriptive than ever before, with reduced attention spans and growing impatience being the norm rather than the exception. This means our ability to capture and retain the attention of our buyers is one of the most significant hurdles to selling. If, however, we develop a method that repeatedly *gains the attention of our buyers*, then we have the starting point of our Unstoppable Sales Machine. In this chapter, we identify exactly how to get and keep the attention of your buyers, building trust and rapport quickly.

HOW BUYERS TODAY ARE LOOKING FOR YOUR PRODUCTS AND SERVICES

When I was 15 and looking to buy my first car, I spent hours reading a black and white print magazine called *Autotrader*. The magazine contained listings of hundreds of cars for sale in my local area, updated weekly. I'd spend hours reading and re-reading those magazines, my hands covered in black newsprint by the end. Each time I found a car that I liked, I'd fold over the corner of the magazine, returning later to revisit the shortlist of vehicles I'd identified.

If I had any questions or wanted to see a car in person, I'd call the number listed to speak with the owner. Then, if the conversation went well and I was still interested, we'd arrange a time to meet for me to look at the car.

I was fortunate to have a friend who was a mechanic who would sometimes travel with me to see a car. Unfortunately, we'd make the drive on

DOI: 10.4324/9781003252641-4

many occasions only to determine that a vehicle had been repainted or repaired after an accident, something the owner often failed to disclose until we pointed out the evidence.

The entire process took a lot of time. As a potential buyer, I had to invest the time to call the seller, arrange a time to view the vehicle that was mutually convenient, arrange for my friend to come with me, and then travel to see the car. In addition to a significant investment of time, the process required that I trust everything a seller told me and invest my time *before* I could ever validate if what they were selling suited my needs, and whether they were trustworthy or not.

Times have changed.

This past summer, I purchased a used Subaru. The entire process was handled entirely online and via telephone. I never visited anyone to view a car, and the first time we met in person was after I had signed a bill of sale and made a deposit. My research didn't consist of any magazines; instead, I used various websites like Autotrader, Kijiji, and Craigslist. I quickly could sort by the model, brand, features, price, color, location, manual vs. automatic, and so on. The list of search options was almost endless. If I chose to do so, it was effortless to view cars outside of my local area, expanding my search nationally and even internationally.

When I found a car I liked, there were often dozens of color pictures to view, a video of the car running, and in some instances, even a 360-degree photo. Not only were there considerably more options to view the vehicle, but there was an option to purchase a Carfax report that would instantly confirm if anyone had ever filed an insurance claim against the car. Considering I had never owned a Subaru, I could quickly look up consumer reports on the quality of the brand and model I was considering buying. Additionally, if I wanted to ensure I was getting a fair price, there are options like Autotrader's Price Indicator or online sites like kellybluebook.com that confirm whether the price is competitive or not.

The entire experience of buying a car in the last 30 years has gone from "I'm looking for a white car" to "I'm looking for a 2017 Subaru WRX Sport-Tech, with under 30,000 miles, in white with leather interior, six-speed transmission and sold by a reputable dealer who will include a warranty."

It's crazy to think about just how much the process has changed.

Considering how different the buying process is today, compared to 30 years ago, it's easy to understand why buyers are more specific in their expectations, and less patient with buying processes that don't meet their expectations. To put it simply, today's buyers want what they want, when they want it, and will only pay what they believe it's worth.

Technology has significantly influenced how we as buyers expect to buy. Likewise, our experiences as consumers (like when we buy a car entirely online) have informed our behaviors and expectations. How we buy as consumers (business to consumer) directly influences our expectations around how we believe in business (business to business).

Let's look at an example.

While advising a client on a sales growth strategy for some new software, they shared their current sales cycle seen in Figure 2.1.

They had about a 20% closing ratio and were spending thousands of dollars on outreach activities, including compensation for several employees involved in the process. When I asked the President what his most significant challenge to generating new sales was, he responded that they were

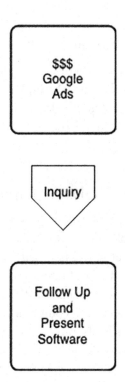

FIGURE 2.1
Sales Process.

spending too much money and time on speaking with people who were never going to buy.

After interviewing some key customers and sitting in on a few sales calls, several problems became immediately apparent:

Problem #1: No Clear Buyer Identified

Although their outreach was successfully driving people to visit their website, the website content itself contained what I call "corporate speak" and didn't clearly define who their services were for and how they solved their problems. As a result, most of the visitors to their site dropped off, choosing not to engage in a call. Additionally, those who agreed to a call were more curious than interested in buying. The vague "corporate speak" on the website had only created confusion for which these visitors had more questions. Unfortunately, despite my clients' best efforts during the calls, confused buyers don't buy, they just ask questions.

Problem #2: Lack of a Clear (and Proven) Sales Process

Among their small sales team, there was no documented sales process. The sales leader trained all their new hires; however, they never provided the employees with any documented sales processes, scripts, or workflows. Essentially, many of the employees on the team were "winging it" when they spoke with a buyer.

Problem #3: No Perceived Value for Buyers

Considering the previous issues, when a buyer did speak with sales, they never received anything of value. Any sales calls that did occur often resulted in the salesperson attempting to sell the buyer on the spot, which in turn lead to brief calls and lack of interest.

These three problems are not unique to this company. In my consulting work I repeatedly connect with companies who are investing heavily in generating inbound sales leads, only to lose those leads once they first engage. Investing in inbound sales without first designing and implementing effective internal sales processes, workflows, and training is a complete waste of money. It's like buying a car without ever looking at pictures, videos, consumer reports, or considering pricing as part of your decision.

THE IMPACT OF ONE CLICK ON BUYER BEHAVIOR

At this point, you're likely wondering why buyer behaviors and expectations have changed so dramatically. After all, we're still human, and the fundamentals of why and how we buy haven't really changed. To begin with the obvious, advancements in technology and the internet have had a direct impact, but it runs deeper than this. There is one significant change we've all experienced (and become accustomed to) that has directly influenced our expectations around the buying experience more than any other: Amazon.

Amazon's one-click buy, that little "buy now" button on the upper right of your screen, has directly influenced our behaviors when making a purchase. The ease with which we can research, validate, and buy on Amazon has directly impacted our expectations around what a buying process should be. Amazon knew this would be the case and even had a patent on the technology until recently.[5]

More specifically, we've learned that any time we make a purchase, it should be:

Self-managed (I can manage the buying process myself).
Effortless (I don't need to jump through hoops to make the buy).
Transparent (It's clear as to what I'm getting and when I'll receive it).
Efficient (I can make the purchase quickly and easily).

When it comes to selling in a B2B environment, for example, although a one-click sale is unlikely, the expectation remains. Remember what I said earlier: our experiences in buying as a consumer (B2C) have directly influenced our expectations around buying in business (B2B).

Despite what you might think, our desire for a quick and efficient buying process extends beyond low value or simple purchases. For example, if you visit Amazon right now, you will find various collectibles up for grabs with price tags close to $1 million. That's million with an M.

A recent McKinsey study[6] shared that B2B buyers today have increased comfort in making large digital purchases online. Over 70% of respondents said they were open to making new, fully self-served, or remote purchases over $50,000. However, 27% would spend more than $500,000.

It's more than just the one-click sale that's influenced buyer behavior. The ease with which we can access information (aka the internet) has also had a significant impact on buying behavior. Consider that when a buyer had a need 20 or even 30 years ago, they searched for a solution in different ways, for example:

1. They defined their problem by discussing it with various people internally and externally.
2. Potential solutions were identified by speaking with peers.
3. The relevance of solutions available was confirmed by meeting with several salespeople.
4. The buyer made a choice relative to the appropriate solution for their issue.
5. The solution they selected was implemented or introduced.
6. After the sale, the buyer determined whether the solution they chose had been effective or not.

Figure 2.2 demonstrates how we tend to make a buy decision based on our personal network.

In this "old way" of buying, the predominance of a buyer's time would be spent in steps #2 and #3, discussing potential solutions with peers, and meeting with salespeople to determine the relevance of their possible solution.

Considering there was no internet (or it was in its infancy), identifying possible solutions would include steps such as:

1. Discussing potential solutions internally with employees.
2. Soliciting recommendations and referrals from one's network.
3. Attending conferences or events to learn about possible solutions.
4. Reviewing past contacts who may have the expertise to help resolve the issue.
5. Meeting with sales professionals based on recommendations of peers.
6. Meeting with sales professionals who reached out cold (and whose solution seemed relevant).
7. Re-connecting with existing suppliers to determine how they might be able to help.

Today, the internet has made accessing potential solutions (and buying in general) so much easier! Just type your problem in Google, and BAM!,

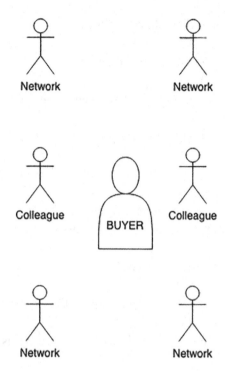

FIGURE 2.2
Buying Based on Personal Network.

you've got pages of answers to your problem (whether the information is relevant or valid is another topic).

Finding potential solutions or options is no longer the time-consuming activity it once was. In fact, now the issue has become information over-whelm. Buyers spend a considerable amount of their time de-mystifying and validating the information they find. Essentially, they spend their time not finding a potential solution but determining what information (and solution) is most relevant.

Referring to our earlier list, #2 and #3 are more accessible than ever to achieve; however, #1 and #4 have become increasingly complex. Why? Buyers spend more time considering the solutions that will best resolve their issues. Specifically, they invest more time clarifying precisely what their problem is and what the best possible solution might be to be sure they identify the correct solution.

Today's buyers spend their time as follows:

- Defining the issue internally with employees (i.e., group discussions, roundtables, etc.).
- Identifying potential solutions with employees (i.e., brainstorming, visioning, etc.).
- Conducting research online for possible solutions (i.e., Google, websites, etc.).
- Conducting research offline for potential solutions (i.e., reports, periodicals, etc.).
- Soliciting recommendations and referrals from one's network.
- Attending events and conferences in person to learn about potential solutions.
- Attending webinars and virtual events to learn about possible solutions.
- Reviewing past suppliers who may have the expertise to help resolve the issue (i.e., email, phone).
- Studying social networks for knowledge or referrals (i.e., LinkedIn).

In addition to time spent on research, buyers must now spend additional time educating and sharing their findings with other decision-makers or influencers, who may have alternate information based on their own research. You can quickly see how difficult it is becoming for today's buyers to buy, which is the very reason why, once a buyer has completed their research and gained internal consensus, **they do not want a complex buying process**.

A recent study by Gartner[7] confirms this shift, finding that buyers today spend nearly 50% of their time in steps #1 through #3 above, but only 17% of their time meeting with sales professionals.

STORIES FROM THE SALES FLOOR

A manufacturing client sought new ways to connect with their buyers and simplify their buying experience. When we looked at their website traffic, we realized that thousands of potential buyers in their region visit their site daily, yet they weren't attempting to interact with them. So, with some hesitation, I convinced them to add a chat module to their website, with someone staffing the chat during regular business hours.

The process was simple: ask website visitors if they had questions, then respond and follow up using an email script. In addition, the scripts presented the option of a follow-up phone call to discuss the visitor's needs. In the first four weeks of the active module, my client made six substantial sales with new customers.

Although this might seem like no big deal, when you consider the company has been around for over 100 years, there aren't many customers they haven't served. Additionally, they had substantial minimum quantities to meet as a manufacturer, yet each customer was willing.

BUILD YOUR UNSTOPPABLE SALES MACHINE

What improvements would your buyers like to see to simplify your buying process further? For your Unstoppable Sales Machine roadmap, visit www.unstoppablesalesmachine.com.

THE ATTENTION GENERATION: HOW TO GET THEIR ATTENTION; KEEP IT; THEN GET IT AGAIN

In the study I referenced previously, Gartner found that today's buyers spend approximately 17% of their time with sales professionals. To be clear, that's not 17% of their time with each salesperson they reach out to; it's the total amount of time they'll spend with all salespeople they decide to engage with.

Suppose we reasonably assume that buyers meet with three different salespeople. In that case, that will leave just over 5% of their time to make an introduction, present your product or service, build a relationship, and discuss any objections or questions they might have.

The only way then to ensure that you get your fair share of time with a buyer is to be clear in what you offer, how you help, and what the next (simple) steps in the buying process are. To put this into context, when I train and coach sales professionals, I often refer to the 8-second rule. As a sales professional you literally have 8 seconds for the buyer to determine if you, your company, and your solution is the right fit for them, or not.

My 8-second rule comes from Microsoft's study several years ago on the impact of technology on our attention span.[8] Although the survey results have been in dispute, the message is loud and clear. Our attention spans diminish as technology continues to feed us information at an increasing pace. To put this into context, not only are today's buyers more explicit in what they expect (being increasingly likely to walk away if they don't think we'll meet their needs), but we have less and less time to convince them we can be of help.

Obtaining 100% of someone's attention is near impossible. Keeping it without being distracted is even more so. For example, if we were in a meeting together, and I was to yell "Fire," how long would you place 100% of your attention with me before you started panicking, asking questions, looking at your phone, or running from the room. It would only be for a matter of seconds, not minutes or hours.

Whether you are calling a buyer on the phone, meeting them in a virtual meeting, trying to engage them with an email, texting them, or using WhatsApp, you only have seconds to get and keep their attention. If you don't capture their interest in 8 seconds, they'll mentally check out and move on.

To get and keep a buyer's attention, we need to consider the initial impression they have when they first engage with us. There are three critical junctures to consider:

1. When they first encounter your company.
2. When they first encounter someone at your company.
3. When they first meet someone in sales.

Let's look at each of these relative to when they apply.

When a Buyer First Encounters Your Company

- Do we understand our buyer and their unique needs?
- Does our product or service appear to satisfy the buyer's expectations?
- Is there proof that we have helped others with similar needs to our buyer?
- Can the buyer easily engage in asking questions (to confirm this)?
- Do we offer value that will help the buyer in their research?

When a Buyer First Engages with Someone at Your Company

- Are there multiple ways to engage (i.e., chat, email, text, phone, etc.)?
- Can the buyer easily engage with a person (not a chatbot or using FAQ)?
- Can the buyer engage with someone quickly?
- Is the person who responds helpful and knowledgeable?
- Do we offer and provide additional resources that will support the buyer?

When a Buyer First Engages with Someone in Sales

- Does the salesperson respond quickly?
- Is the salesperson friendly, knowledgeable, helpful, responsive?
- Does the salesperson smile, engage through eye contact, use an upbeat tone of voice?
- Is the salesperson an expert at using language to guide the conversation?
- Does the salesperson follow up as promised and promptly?

Of all three of these points of contact above, area #3 is the most important. A strong sales professional can often overcome weaknesses in the other two areas. However, if these areas are weak, your sales team will often lose the opportunity to engage with a buyer, as their attention is lost, and they move on to the next company.

For several years my wife and I drove Nissans, in part for the service we received from one person. The first time the salesperson walked me back to service and introduced me to Sheryl, she immediately asked if I had leased the car or purchased it. When I told her we had leased it, she immediately recommended we don't follow the typical vehicle service plan because the investment wouldn't make sense if we weren't planning to keep the car.

Sheryl immediately added value as a new customer through that simple, friendly interaction and ultimately sold me on four years of service. After a few years, Sheryl left the dealership, and I moved my service to a local mechanic. The main reason we moved on is that Sheryl was the reason I took my car to the dealership. She was always friendly; ensured she presented us with convenient times for maintenance; and communicated in ways that worked for us (text, email, phone, depending on what was most accessible for us). The list goes on, but you get the point.

As a result of Sheryl's efforts, she (and the dealership) made thousands of dollars in fees and commissions. Moreover, Sheryl treated everyone this way, so the impact on the business was significant.

If you want to get and keep your buyer's attention, you need to be strong in all three of the areas. Doing so will not only provide you more opportunities to sell, but you'll stand out head and shoulders above your competition because few companies can do this well.

BUILD YOUR UNSTOPPABLE SALES MACHINE

What is the buyer's first impression when they reach out to your company? For your Unstoppable Sales Machine roadmap, visit www.unstoppablesalesmachine.com.

SOLVING A PROBLEM IS NOT THE PROBLEM

Buyers today aren't seeking to solve a problem. In most instances, they already know (or at least have some ideas around) how to solve the problem. Instead, they want to engage with companies that can add value, helping them navigate the plethora of solutions to find the best fit for their specific needs.

If you do gain the attention and interest of a buyer, then you need to set yourself apart from the competition. Consider that there are likely several companies that offer similar products or services as you do. When a buyer first encounters your company, even if they have a positive initial encounter, you need to capture (and keep) their attention. You do this by offering value that will improve your customer's situation.

Customers don't buy cybersecurity services; they buy peace of mind.

Customers don't buy a new piece of equipment; they buy increased revenue.

Customers don't buy financial services; they buy increased profitability or reduced expenses.

Customers don't buy a new widget; they buy a unique market opportunity.

The greater your ability to add value that helps your buyer, the better your chances of making a sale.

The question we must ask ourselves then is what do my buyers value? Some reasonable assumptions might include time, accessibility, helpful information, responsiveness, and so on. But we need to dive deeper and place value at the forefront of our approach to how we engage with and sell to our buyers.

The following five questions will help you to identify what value your buyers might expect or appreciate:

1. What does your customer need? What is their current situation?
2. Why do they need this? Why is now the right time?
3. How does your product or service improve their current situation?
4. How is your product or service different from your competitors?
5. Why should they choose your product or service over the competitors?

Although the concept of value-based selling has been around for some time, many of my clients fail to take a systematic approach to add value to their buyer's journey. We'll dive deeper into defining value for your buyer, and how to effectively deliver that value in the upcoming chapters.

STORIES FROM THE SALES FLOOR

When I was helping a client expand their business in Mexico, we first spent considerable time interviewing, speaking with, and visiting target accounts in regions such as Monterrey and Queretaro, where they wanted to expand. Next, we focused on identifying what buyers in each of these regions valued and how this may differ from buyers in other countries, for example:

- What were the standard practices buyers used to connect with new suppliers?
- What were the preferred methods to communicate?
- How did buyers typically research new suppliers?
- What were they seeking once they found them?
- What did existing suppliers to the buyer offer that was deemed beneficial?
- What were the qualifying factors that buyers considered as necessary?

These might seem more like exploratory sales questions; however, in every instance, what we were looking for is exactly how my client could add value that would enable them to get the attention of (and ultimately sell more to) existing and new buyers in Mexico.

After three separate trips, we identified an approach to selling and expanding their business in these regions in Mexico that would satisfy the expectations of their buyers and place them ahead of their competition (many of whom had never traveled to the region or made the effort to meet with buyers in person). Some examples of the changes included recognizing the importance of:

- Having a version of their website available in Spanish.
- Using WhatsApp as a primary communication tool with buyers.
- Changing hours of sales staff to align with the different time zones.
- Using video as a primary means of communicating the unique attributes of my client's products, and their processes.
- Having a presence (or person) in Mexico to continue building relationships.

What's important to recognize here is that my client's pricing (or pricing competitiveness) was never a factor. None of the conversations we had with existing and potential buyers discussed my client's pricing. Instead, we were focused on how we could add value and set my client apart from their competitors.

This is an important point to mention. Regardless of what you sell, price becomes less of an important factor if (and when) you lead with value throughout the buyer's journey.

Where quality and price are equal, buyers decide where and how they'll invest based on the value they receive.

Let me give you an example.

My father had been experiencing leaks in his garage and decided it was likely time to get a new roof. He contacted three companies that were reputable and known in his area. The first company never returned his call; the second company gave him a price over the phone without ever seeing his house or roof; the third company, one of the busiest in the area, dropped by a day later and asked if they could go up and look at the roof.

Once he was on the roof, the contractor noticed cracks leading to the leaks my Dad had experienced. So he went to his truck to grab some sealant and returned to the roof without saying a word, applying the product to every crack he found.

Although this contractor had a higher price than one of the other companies, who do you think my Dad happily awarded the contract to?

> **BUILD YOUR UNSTOPPABLE SALES MACHINE**
>
> Answer the previous five questions and ask yourself how you can introduce value throughout your buyer's journey. For your Unstoppable Sales Machine roadmap, visit www.unstoppablesalesmachine. com.

IMPATIENCE IS THE NEW NORM: HOW TIME CAN MAKE OR BREAK THE SALE

If you've captured your buyer's attention, and you're providing them with significant value, there is another key differentiator you'll need to incorporate. With so little of a buyer's time available and such a short attention span, you need to service your buyers with speed.

As Nathan Bedford Forrest, lieutenant-general in the confederate army once said, "*You need to get there first with the most. . . .*"

Consider the last time you made a purchase of any kind. Groceries, lawn care services, even a carwash. Were you prepared to wait patiently to make the purchase? The short answer is no. Gone are the days of customers waiting patiently in a waiting room or on the phone.

I realize that from a business standpoint, supporting a "*we're ready when you are*" approach to connecting with your buyers can be costly and difficult to implement. It's the reason why you'll most often receive a message while calling your phone company or bank that says, "*Call volumes are higher than normal. We apologize for any inconvenience.*"

In most instances, companies could hire more people to manage fluctuations in inbound calls; however, it might mean that due to unpredictability, some employees would be sitting waiting on calls. Of course, no one wants to pay an employee to sit around, but in many instances, that's what they should be doing if they're going to gain the attention and interest of today's time-sensitive buyers.

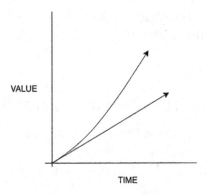

FIGURE 2.3
Time Has Value.

As seen in Figure 2.3, time impacts the perception of value. The faster we receive a response, the more time we are willing to invest in a conversation and the more excellent value we perceive in the interaction.

In essence, speed = value.

Today's buyers spend so little time with sales professionals that we need to ensure that every interaction with them quickly provides value. The best way to do so is by using speed as our differentiator. We need to "get there first, with the most."

I've glazed over these three important areas in this chapter, just to give you some ideas around how you can best attract, serve, and support buyers today. They go much deeper than we've discussed here, and we'll spend time in future chapters discussing exactly how you can introduce these important components, as part of your Unstoppable Sales Machine. For now, just know that these are areas you'll need to tackle if you truly want to generate more sales.

BUILD YOUR UNSTOPPABLE SALES MACHINE ACTION STEP

What are the points at which potential buyers might engage with your company? How quickly does your team respond? How can you improve response times in each of these areas? For your Unstoppable Sales Machine roadmap, visit www.unstoppablesalesmachine.com.

3

Be There First with the Most: Staying Ahead of Your Competition

There is no second place in sales. You either win the sale, or your competitor does. To stay ahead of the competition, you need to build a proven and repeatable system to generate sales. In this chapter, we'll discuss what you need to construct your very own Unstoppable Sales Machine and start generating repeatable and predictable sales.

CUSTOMER INTELLIGENCE: ZIG WHEN YOUR COMPETITORS ZAG

When it comes to staying ahead of the competition, you'll need to equip yourself with competitive intelligence repeatedly. The frequency with which you collect this information, and more importantly, its accuracy, is vital to your success. A recent study conducted by Forrester for Zoominfo found that only 8% of sales professionals say that their (sales) data is over 91% accurate.[9] Collecting competitive intelligence (and customer intelligence, which we'll discuss later) isn't something most companies are good at, yet this information is vital to the effectiveness of your Unstoppable Sales Machine, so let's start here.

It's impossible to make informed decisions on finding and selling to customers if the intelligence and information collected is inaccurate (or nonexistent!). Furthermore, you can't afford to make decisions without basing them on current, relevant information about your customers, competitors, and the market. If you do, you're risking any (or all) of the following:

DOI: 10.4324/9781003252641-5

- Selling a product or service that is over-priced for the market.
- Selling a product or service that is under-priced (and leaving money on the table).
- Wasting your sales team's time chasing buyers that aren't ready or willing to buy.
- Attempting to sell a solution that your ideal buyers don't deem helpful or valuable.
- Reducing the capacity of your sales team who (with better information) could sell more.
- Wasting money on attending events that don't contain your ideal buyers.

Collecting and using poor data is more common than you might think. For this reason, one of the first actions I take when working with new clients is to speak directly to their customers as part of my Customer Comprehension Survey. There is no better way to ensure the accuracy of your competitive and customer intelligence than by speaking to customers (existing, past, and future) directly. Moreover, when this is done by a third party (rather than your own salespeople) it can provide additional value and insights that may have otherwise gotten lost in translation.

The Customer Comprehension Survey intends to collect relevant and timely intelligence while informing the customer (indirectly) of additional buying opportunities. This method of gathering customer intelligence can serve several purposes, including:

1. Identify why existing customers buy from you and your company.
2. Foresee opportunities to sustain and retain key customer accounts.
3. Confirm opportunities to help to close sales faster.
4. Capture specific feedback on the value of working with you or your company, providing material for customer testimonials.
5. Determine what other products or services you might offer (gaps in the market).
6. Identify opportunities to introduce other (existing) products or services to customers.
7. Capture customer intelligence that is current, relevant, and applicable.

In my experience, you can't identify opportunities to sell more if you don't first connect with existing customers to gather intelligence. It would be akin to trying to make healthier eating choices without first speaking to a dietitian; or trying to get your car to run better without having a technician look it over first.

You can always do this research yourself, but I recommend having a credible third party complete it as you'll gain insights that might otherwise be dismissed. After all, if you could do this effectively with your internal resources, wouldn't your sales team already be bringing you timely and relevant insights from customers? If they aren't, consider initiating a third party to assist you and create a basis point upon which we'll be making decisions around building your Unstoppable Sales Machine.

Collecting intelligence in this comprehensive way extends beyond just the insights you can gain to help you to sell more. For example, in the preceding approach, you'll notice that there are also opportunities to sell more products or services customers may not have purchased from you yet. Additionally, you can identify and ward off any circumstances in which customers may be displeased with your products or services and consider buying from someone else.

I recommend all my clients apply the **Customer Comprehension Survey** every quarter, using the following ten steps:

1. Select five customer accounts—a combination of long-time and new customers.
2. Identify the critical decision-maker within each account.
3. Organize a brief 20-minute conversation with the decision-maker.
4. Ask a series of questions to solicit direct feedback.
5. Capture feedback in your CRM and a separate document for review internally.
6. After the discussion, send your customer a token of your appreciation.
7. Analyze customer feedback to identify trends and opportunities.
8. Review the feedback with your sales and marketing teams to confirm the next steps.
9. Complete this activity every 3 months.
10. Track all internal actions to completion and follow up promptly with any customers based on feedback or concerns identified.

BUILD YOUR UNSTOPPABLE SALES MACHINE

If you'd like a simple printable version of the Customer Comprehension Survey, visit www.untoppablesalesmachine.com.

STORIES FROM THE SALES FLOOR

I completed a Customer Comprehension Survey for a SAAS (software as a service) client looking to double their sales. Using the previously outlined steps, I reached out to a half-dozen clients to gain some intelligence that would inform some changes in how they marketed their services. Four out of six customers I spoke with repeatedly spoke of the value of working with the company. When I asked if they would refer other companies to use my clients, their overwhelming response was "absolutely."

After completing the survey, I met with my client to review the results, during which I asked, "Do you have a referral process in place?" After looking at the floor for a moment, my client said, "No, why?" I shared feedback from his customers on their overwhelming desire to refer other businesses his way. "Do I need a referral process for them to offer referrals?" he asked . . .

Note: If you have customers who are excited about your products and services and are willing to refer others to you, you need to give them a simple process for doing so. We'll discuss a way for you to develop and introduce one in the upcoming chapters.

I suggested to my client that he would likely double his sales if he asked every customer to provide him with one referral every 3 months. Assuming a 25% closing ratio (which is low!), he would, at a minimum, add 25% new business every 3 months. Not a bad return for asking a question, something that he would never have considered had I not reached out and spoken to his customers.

WHY ELECTRONIC SURVEYS ARE A WASTE OF TIME

When I speak about using a **Customer Comprehension Survey**, many of the executives and sales leaders I meet with often suggest things like *"Oh, we have a Net Promoter Survey already,"* or *"We send out a customer survey annually already."* My response—you should stop wasting your time and money.

In my opinion, electronic surveys are worthless.

Think about the last time *you* answered an electronic survey. I guess it was because one of two situations existed: either you were so happy with the product or service that you wanted to tell the world—or you were so disappointed that you tried to ensure someone knew. When things were "good enough," you likely didn't see value in investing the time in every other situation.

Moreover, electronic surveys don't allow an opportunity to explore responses. There's too much ambiguity between individual answers to the questions and the person interpreting how they respond. If, for example, I asked you to rate your experience on a scale of 1 to 10, where 10 is "Excellent," and you scored me a 10, is there nothing to be improved? What made the experience or purchase a 10? What would make it a 1?

If you're going through the effort of collecting data, select a smaller sample size and then use a personalized interaction to explore responses, gain clarity on feedback, and solicit additional questions when it makes sense. It's the only way to ensure the responses and feedback are truly understood.

If you have current and relevant customer intelligence in hand, you are in the best position to take the next step in preparing to build your Unstoppable Sales Machine, creating alignment between your marketing and sales teams using a hybrid selling methodology.

THE HYBRID SELLING: SALES AND MARKETING WORKING TOGETHER

Referring to our earlier discussions, considering today's buyers spend 50% of their time researching BEFORE they engage with sales, we need to start thinking about the roles of sales and marketing, and how they work together, differently.

Gone are the days of marketing developing a list of inquiries (notice I didn't call these leads) and tossing them over the wall to sales. It's wasteful and does nothing for the morale of marketing (when they hear their efforts to generate leads haven't led to new sales), and it wastes the time of sales, who quickly become frustrated with the poor quality of information.

Does any of this sound familiar? If you want to create an Unstoppable Sales Machine for your company, you'll need to build a more strategic collaboration between sales and marketing. I call this Hybrid Selling, the application of which can rapidly increase the speed, quality, and ability to close new deals.

Let's start then by discussing what hybrid selling is and isn't.

Hybrid Selling is the strategic collaboration between sales and marketing, measured by the quality of leads and volume and size of the deals closed. It's connecting what are considered two very different disciplines, understanding that the common theme between sales and marketing is to find, convert, and close high-quality, repeatable customers.

Marketing is not about producing likes and shares. Instead, its primary role is to ensure we attract ideal buyers who are ready to engage. As a result, the quality and quantity of leads that marketing generates become the foundational measures for our marketing.

Additionally, when we align our sales and marketing teams, we can hold sales accountable for their results because we know the quality of the leads they are receiving is high.

If you're still not convinced of the need for marketing and sales to align in their efforts closely, then let's revisit my earlier point about the recent Gartner study. It suggested that today's buyers are spending 50% of their time, or more, researching a product or service BEFORE they engage with sales. Marketing is typically on the front lines of providing the information to entice a buyer to research.

But let's flip this around for a moment. Suppose as a sales professional, you are at a tradeshow and meet a potential buyer. You might argue that marketing doesn't enter the equation if sales meets a buyer before conducting any research. Well, let me ask you. When you meet someone for the first time in a business environment, what's the first thing you do if you are interested in what they are selling? I would guess that you go online to check out their company website, LinkedIn profile, and anything else that might seem relevant. But meeting a buyer can often entice them to research to confirm who you are and if you offer what you say you do.

Sales' success (or lack thereof) is directly proportional to how effective marketing is. You can't sell (or reach the level of unstoppable sales) without having effective marketing in place. Of course, you can try, but it will take you longer, and eventually, your ability to acquire new sales will diminish.

Case Study: More Sales Result When More Buyers Know You

The President of an MSP (Managed Service Provider) company approached me. Over the last several years, their business had grown steadily; however, within the last 12 months, sales had plateaued.

Considering the power of their customer relationships, we introduced several methods to begin capturing and sharing their client testimonials with potential buyers. These included sharing on social media, in sales presentations, and email signatures; we also equipped their sales team with various print and digital versions for distribution, added them to the bottom of their proposals, invoices, and even on the back of business cards and sales brochures. Everywhere the sales team went, they took with them glowing testimonials.

After four weeks, new inbound inquiries and leads began to present themselves, allowing my client to close new sales and slowly increase their MRR (monthly reoccurring revenue). Within 3 months, they had doubled their inbound lead volume, with higher quality leads that allowed them to generate more revenue.

As you can tell, there are many benefits to using Hybrid Selling, not the least of which include:

1. **Clarity on who your ideal buyer is**. We ensure that our marketing is effective, resulting in sales receiving leads that align with our objectives.
2. **Increased focus on activities that generate the most interest from ideal buyers**. Hybrid Selling brings marketing and sales together on deciding what actions it will take to gain the most selling opportunities. Rather than working independently, both groups decide on the ideal opportunities based on their collective intelligence and experience.
3. **Better use of sales time and capacity**. With our sales and marketing teams aligned, generating sales becomes a mutual focus, resulting in more efficient use of both marketing and sales time. No more arguing over the quality of leads marketing provides; or sales not following up on the leads that marketing provides. Mutually aligned goals means less resistance and greater momentum toward the goal . . . more sales!
4. **Laser-like focus on activities that generate results**. With both sales and marketing aligned, making decisions on things like campaigns, events, or exhibits becomes less vague and highly focused on ensuring sales get in front of the right people, at the right time and place.
5. **Long-term selling success**. There is an ongoing collaboration between sales and marketing in a hybrid selling model. As a result,

any improvements or adjustments made to ongoing campaigns and activities are introduced quickly and met with open arms and encouragement—rather than complaints and discouragement.

See Figure 3.1 for an overview of Hybrid Selling.

Lisa Shepherd is the President of Mezzanine, B2B Growth Agents. Lisa and her team work with companies who sell business to business, helping them to introduce and implement digital marketing growth strategies. I spoke with Lisa about her advice for companies looking to grow.

> Traditional B2B companies who have been generating sales from just their sales team have a huge opportunity to generate new deals using digital marketing strategies. Done correctly, these strategies can extend their reach to a much broader audience, and when aligned with effective sales strategies, growth is imminent.

Lisa also mentioned that the key is to have realistic expectations about how long digital marketing strategies will take to yield results. "You should see leads within 6 to 12 months' time, and direct revenue within 6 to 24 months, depending on the typical sales cycle for your products and

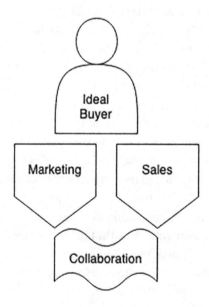

FIGURE 3.1
Hybrid Selling.

services." The key then, according to Lisa, is to stick with your digital marketing strategy and ensure that your sales team works in conjunction with your digital strategy to capture the new lead and revenue opportunities.

This is hybrid selling at its best.

TOOLS YOU'LL NEED TO MAKE YOUR MACHINE SING

The processes and resources you'll put into practice to create your Unstoppable Sales Machine will require that you develop some new processes, develop some new skills, and have a willingness to adopt some technology. It's this last one that people often get tripped up on, believing that an Unstoppable Sales *Machine* is some sort of fully automated technology. It's not, and you don't need to be a technology wizard to build your machine. Instead, the key is to select technology that suits your needs.

Considering it's easy to get sucked into the idea that software can resolve all your sales problems *and* help you sell more (spoiler alert, it can't), let's start with discussing some of the most basic technology you'll likely need as part of your machine. Keep in mind this is very personal to your company, size, market, product, or service, and so on.

Having highly complex and expensive CRM (Customer Relationship Management) software to track leads, actions, and conversations is not always necessary for a sales team to be effective. On the flip side, however, just using a spreadsheet or free CRM software might not be sufficient either. As Abraham Maslow once said, "*. . . if the only tool you have is a hammer, you treat everything as if it were a nail.*"

In my experience, I've seen too many sales leaders use their CRM software as an excuse for poor sales results. Reasons include software being too complex, difficult, or cumbersome to use.

Instead, you should select software that supports your sales processes. So, before you get upsold on the idea (by a good salesperson selling CRM software!) that a CRM or other software will help you sell more, let's prioritize your specific needs.

Let's take a few minutes then to outline some of the most common (and important) software you'll want to consider as part of your Unstoppable Sales Machine, placing these in order of importance to focus your efforts on generating new and repeated sales, rather than on some new bright and shiny technology that will (apparently) do everything for you (remember what I mentioned earlier . . . it won't).

1. Customer Relationship Management (CRM) Software

I mentioned earlier that CRM is not the only tool for sales today, and that's true. But most of today's CRM software can do so much more than track names and notes. Unfortunately, in my experience, companies today either have an insufficient CRM or they've purchased the most extensive (and expensive) system they can buy, which is too much for their needs, often resulting in technology overwhelm.

You'll need your CRM software to be capable of a few simple things, namely:

- Capture all contact information, including name (multiple), company, website, address, email, phone number at minimum.
- Allow for call recording (for training purposes and to capture internal best practices).
- Provide areas for logging notes, last contact points, and next steps.
- Connect with internal calendars to track meetings.
- Have reporting capabilities that identify new business status, activity, pipeline health, etc. (we'll discuss this more in the metrics section later).

2. Customer Engagement Channels

My mentor, Alan Weiss, once said, "you never know where your next lead will come from." Therefore, to ensure that you are ready to capture all inbound inquiries, you'll need various channels for inbound communication that are set up and monitored 24/7.

These channels should include (at a minimum) the following:

- Telephone number prominently displayed on all customer-facing materials and platforms.
- Email address prominently displayed on all customer-facing materials and platforms.

- Webchat that is monitored and responded to within 2 minutes during regular business hours (after-hours should have the option to add a note or question and be responded to within 30 minutes of opening the following day).
- A contact form on your website that is easily found and doesn't require 20 steps to send a message. The gold standard here is to allow for both a contact form AND an email address for written contact.
- Text inquiries and questions. Created using your existing phone number (if it allows for texting), or you can add software such as Textedly (www.texedly.com) or Twilio (www.twilio.com). As more of today's younger generations prefer to engage by instant message, texting becomes a channel you need to open up potential new buyers.
- Fax, although extremely outdated, is still a preference for how some buyers and their companies prefer to engage. Although I don't consider this channel mandatory, if your buyers would like to use a fax channel, then it's something you should have in place.
- WhatsApp has become a platform that many buyers enjoy engaging on, particularly in some countries like Mexico, where it is the preferred means to communicate. Like faxing, determine if your ideal buyers prefer to use WhatsApp or another similar SMS platform and if they do, make sure you offer it.

3. A Functioning Website

It's no surprise that you'll need a website if you want to build an Unstoppable Sales Machine. Your website is a means to an end, not an end in and of itself. The purpose of any website is to encourage and empower a buyer to buy. Period, end of the story. It's not about displaying every aspect of your business, technology, awards, and so on. We need to stop thinking about a website as an online directory of our services (that's what online directories are for!). Instead, it is a tool to attract our ideal buyers to our solutions when researching. The main aspects of your website then should include:

- Language that speaks directly to the challenges and needs of your buyer.
- Answers to their questions prominently displayed at the top of the page (without scrolling).

- Clear contact information that is prominently displayed.
- A live webchat that engages them while they are on-page.
- Free resources that will support them during their research.
- No more than three calls to action throughout the site that capture their contact information.

4. Video Platforms

When you consider how much time today's buyers spend researching, it only makes sense that you will want to emphasize creating personalized interactions as much as possible during this phase. Of course, you can do this directly through your sales team but want to create videos that offer support when the buyer may not have engaged yet. Some examples of the most common video platforms and uses to create an Unstoppable Sales Machine are as follows:

1. Videos on your website explain your solution and how it will help your ideal buyer.
2. External platforms like YouTube or Vimeo allow your sales team to create videos to answer the most common questions they hear from buyers.
3. Videos used in conjunction with email create a more personalized interaction (i.e., www.bombbomb.com or www.loom.com).

Before you run out and begin selecting or introducing software, it's important that you complete the following steps.

1. Document your internal processes to capture best practices; use this information to identify how software is introduced and used (see my example of why this is important later).
2. Clear metrics to measure the success of each piece of software; if you introduce software that does not have a positive impact on your sales team or customers, why use it?
3. Relevant training that ensures everyone using the software understands how and when to best use the software.

We'll discuss these further in the upcoming chapters, but for now just keep in mind that the goal isn't to use software for software's sake. I've seen high-performing sales teams get by using an Excel spreadsheet to monitor/ capture their business leads. The primary goal is always to better serve our customer, followed by improving our own internal efficiency and capabilities. Start small and seek to outgrow the software you're using before you consider upgrading or adding the next best thing.

Case Study: Hidden Customer Files

A $50M manufacturer of clothing was losing customers. There were mixed messages being received from customers, leading to confusion on what improvements were necessary to improve the customers' experience. The President was constantly surprised that feedback the customer service team received from a customer didn't align with what sales was saying about the same customer. When the President would ask sales how their customer visits went it was typically very positive. However, if they went to discuss something about that same customer with customer service, they would often get a very different picture of the relationship.

After speaking with several employees on the sales and customer service teams, it became apparent that there were several issues at hand. First, sales and customer service were often speaking to two different departments, resulting in very different feedback. Any feedback each department received was being documented in their own customer file, not accessible by the other department. Lastly, there were no shared files or communications between the two departments around customer feedback.

We introduced some simple CRM software for all customer notes to be captured in and launched weekly meetings between sales and customer service to share updates on customer discussions. These two simple changes resulted in greater clarity around customer feedback, which in turn informed improvements the manufacturer needed to make to provide a better customer experience. Within 3 months they had avoided the loss of three different customers just by making these changes alone.

Just like a mechanic can't repair your car without the right tools, sales can't be effective without the right tools that align and inform their discussions and interactions with buyers.

EMPOWERING YOUR BUYERS TO BUY

When I was younger, I spent a portion of my holidays at my Gramma and Grampa's house. They lived in a small community of about 50 people, and the door into their carport was always left open. When I asked my Grampa why he left the doors open, he said it dated back to when his kids were younger and lived at home. Leaving the doors unlocked meant that if someone needed to get in late at night, they wouldn't have to wake anyone up to do so.

Although times may have changed, we need to think about our buyers in this same manner, as welcomed guests in our home. When connecting with buyers, we always need to leave our doors open and unlocked, figuratively speaking. What this means is that we always need to be:

- Accessible after hours (phone service, chat, email response, text response).
- Ready to provide quotes or proposals after hours (if that's what a buyer wants).
- Able to process and commence customer orders after hours.

Whether a buyer lands on our website, happens across our social media, lands on a report or case study that we published, or finds an article that features our product or service, who knows.

That's the point—who knows how our ideal buyer will first encounter our company, product, or service? As today's buyers spend less and less time engaging with sales professionals and more and more time researching, we need to ensure that:

1. They can find us everywhere they might be looking for our product, service, or solution.
2. When they do, it's crystal clear that we understand their needs, and we can help.
3. There are multiple ways they can connect with us quickly and easily.

If you've introduced the tools and software we discussed earlier, you've already laid the groundwork for creating this kind of accessibility. If not, what are you waiting for?

It's typically at this point you might be wondering to what degree do you need to be available for your buyers. Is this a 24/7/365 thing, or just during regular business hours? The answer will really depend on your buyers' preferences. To determine then when and what your buyers might need access to from your company, start by asking a select few of your existing customers the following questions:

1. When you seek a solution like ours, where do you look for answers?
2. When do you typically find the time to seek solutions to your most significant challenges?
3. What kinds of resources, information, or support would be helpful to you during this phase?
4. What is your preferred format for this information or help?
5. What would make this research more straightforward for you and a no-brainer to move forward?

Responses to these questions will help you quickly identify and prioritize what you need to provide access to, and when. But, more importantly, you can strategize about best engaging your ideal buyers when and where they want to hire.

To be clear, you don't need to engage with customers at all hours of the night, but you do need to think strategically about how your buyer prefers to engage. For example, consider their preferred means of communication; expectations around responsiveness; and so on. Consider, for example, that if I need to e-transfer money, it might be at any time, including 2 am on a Saturday. Alternatively, I may periodically need a certified check; however, it would be far less frequent and most likely during daytime hours.

Using this information to build your sales machine empowers your buyers to buy. You ensure that your entire company is ready to engage with your ideal buyer at the right time and place.

There's nothing worse than hearing a potential buyer pass over your company, its products, or services simply because they found what they needed somewhere else. For that reason, you must keep your doors open to engaging with your potential buyers when, where, and how they'd like to engage.

A former client of mine, Upper Canada Stretcher, was manufacturing and selling products globally for years. Orders arrived via telephone or web contact form and would trickle inconsistently. However, their sales took off when they created an online commerce platform, coupled with robust diagrams and specifications around their existing products. They empowered their customers to buy, providing the information and ability to purchase without ever engaging anyone.

The key is this: if you want to build an Unstoppable Sales Machine, you'll need to create strong internal collaborations to ensure your customer-facing roles work together to attract, convert, and close your ideal buyers. To aid their efforts, you'll need to select and introduce the right technology and be prepared to connect with your ideal buyers when and where they want. These two changes alone are the key ingredients to empowering your customers to buy from you.

4

What Will Happen If You Don't Build Your Sales Machine?

Let me be honest with you for a moment. If you're thinking of building your Unstoppable Sales Machine, it'll likely require that you make some changes in how you attract, convert, and close new buyers, and change, of any magnitude, is difficult. As a result, you may be questioning why you need to build an Unstoppable Sales Machine at all. After all, if your sales are relatively consistent, why would any of this effort make sense? I can tell you from experience, if you don't, there's a good chance that the proverbial rug is going to be pulled out from under you in short order.

Sound like a scare tactic? It's not. Despite the degree of success you have with generating new sales, things change often without warning. Just look at how many companies had their sales cease immediately in the 2008/9 financial crisis or in 2020 when the pandemic took hold.

This chapter will explore how continued shifts in the market will impact your ability to sell and how your Unstoppable Sales Machine will provide you with the insurance and peace of mind you need to survive and thrive amidst these changes.

STRONG SALES DON'T LAST FOREVER

I will never forget the time I called the owner of a large manufacturing company whom I'd met at a recent event. Inspired by his company's growth, I reached out and suggested we set up a time to speak (I'm always looking to connect with and learn from those who are seeing great success in sales).

DOI: 10.4324/9781003252641-6

After some small talk, the CEO said the following, and I quote, "*Shawn, I appreciate the call but have to be honest with you. The last thing we need right now is more sales. Our backlogs are out eight weeks, and we can't keep up.*"

Despite the truth to his statement, let me ask you, if you take the focus off generating new sales, because of capacity issues, supply chain issues, or staffing issues, how difficult is it to ramp up selling activities again once these situations have passed? What if they don't get resolved? Are you prone to limp along at mediocre sales for the rest of your career? Let me be the first to suggest to you that you should never, ever stop focusing on generating new sales. That's why I designed the Unstoppable Sales Machine, to keep your sales team focused on generating new sales (regardless of factors around them) yet allow you some degree of control over the volume of sales you generate. More on this in upcoming chapters.

In my experience, if your sales are strong, investing any effort or time in introducing an Unstoppable Sales Machine might seem like a waste. The laws of atrophy, however, tell us that over time, randomness, chaos, disorder, and randomly occurring events in the universe will result in a gradual decline in sales. If those statements are too woo-woo for you, then let me put it another way: what goes up must come down, and introducing an Unstoppable Sales Machine is the only way to ensure you don't experience the "down."

Looking at Figure 4.1, you'll notice precisely how sales tend to rise and fall over time. I call this Sales Bell Curve.

You might be wondering exactly how sales will erode if the factors that could influence a drop in sales aren't clear to you at this moment. Unlike

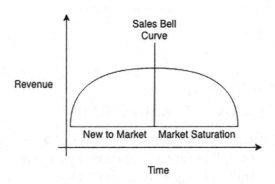

FIGURE 4.1
Sales Bell Curve.

the catastrophic events I referenced earlier, the more common way sales erode isn't a one-time event but rather a slow decline in demand that happens over time, often going unnoticed until too late. Think of it like a river that slowly erodes the riverbank over time. The most public examples I can share are companies like Compaq computers, Pan Am Airways, and Toys"R"Us, which are all examples of how a slow erosion of sales can lead to the demise of a company.

The idea of erosion may not be a concern for you right now. Typically, we like to believe that if something is going to decline, it's the direct result of a single impact or issue. However, in my experience consulting and coaching organizations and their leaders for nearly 20 years, I can tell you from experience that a decline in sales rarely ever boils down to one specific problem or issue.

For example, you might believe that low sales result from an underperforming employee. However, once you improve that employee's skills through sales coaching or training, you're likely to find there are other factors at play. For example, mastery of other sales professionals on the team, the technology you're using to enable the sales team's effectiveness, how closely aligned marketing and sales are, and so on.

Some examples of influences that can erode your sales today include:

1. **Global Economic Changes**: A continued expansion of the global economy means more competition for the same customers. Although Netflix may have put Blockbuster out of business, today Disney+, HBO, Prime, and others are slowly eroding Netflix's market share. They've increased their prices to remain profitable, but unless they continue to introduce new and unique value that sets them apart from the competition, their sales will erode over time.

2. **Influence of Technology on the Buying Process**: As we've discussed previously, today's buyers have an increasing level of comfort (and expectations) around the use of e-commerce. This shift creates a digital-first approach to sales, allowing buyers a greater sense of control over the buying process. A recent article in Forbes[10] confirms that today's buyers want to skip the introductory buyer meeting and instead have sellers that help them navigate their education around a product or service. This digital-first approach means that the role of sales professionals and reps needs to change if sales are to remain strong.

3. **Shifting Buyer Demographics**: As the age and demographic of today's buyers continue to change, how we sell needs to align with buyer preferences. It should be no surprise that younger generations such as Millennials or Gen Z prefer to research and buy online rather than pick up the phone to make a call. Ensuring the buyer experience aligns with this change in demographic preferences means continued opportunities to sell rather than losing sales to the competition.

4. **Evolution of Organizational Decision-Making**: A recent Forrester study[11] identified a shift in buyer preference to make decisions based on group involvement and input in the buying decision. Although one person may still hold the final say in making the purchase, they're increasingly seeking broader information from co-workers and team members before making this decision.

5. **Preference for a Self-Managed Buying Process**: Forrester also concluded that the number of self-guided buyer interactions (a buyer reaching out to discuss their products or services) has jumped from 17 to 27 interactions *before they ever make a buying decision*. Put differently, the number of times buyers need to engage before finalizing a buying decision has jumped dramatically, leading to lengthier buying cycles. In addition, as buyers move on to different roles, new buyers (who do not have the same relationships) are more likely to do more research and outreach before making a buying decision. Do you see the risk this can create for your sales?

These are just a few examples of how buyer behaviors and preferences evolve. However minuscule they may seem, not preparing for and adapting to these shifts and changes *proactively* is akin to death by 1000 cuts.

DEATH BY 1000 CUTS: THE WRONG APPROACH TO SELLING

If your sales are strong, or even if they aren't, the first step to introducing your Unstoppable Sales Machine is to change your philosophy around how new sales are generated. In my experience, there are predominantly five different approaches to selling that are ingrained in a company's culture, often based on the beliefs and preferences of the owner or leaders within the organization.

Knowing which approach your company uses today will help you identify how to transition to a philosophy of generating unstoppable sales. So, let's dive in and look at each approach, its pros, and cons, and the specific starting point to transition toward introducing your Unstoppable Sales Machine.

Approach #1: "Build It, and They Will Come" Sales Model

A couple of years ago, I worked with a software company. The company had successfully built custom software for years that had provided tremendous value to their clients. They decided to develop some new software that they were confident would be helpful to their customers.

They painstakingly worked on developing the software for over a year, testing, improving, and validating it. Then, with the software near complete and ready for the market, the company began to study the market to identify who might be interested in buying the software.

It's the old "build it, and they will come" approach to selling, and it's rarely successful.

Unfortunately, however, I run into this all the time. Companies who have a product or service believe they have a massive hit on their hands, and they'll be the next Apple or Uber, only to realize after many failed attempts and spending a lot of money that no one wants what they have to offer. So, let's look at the pros and cons of this approach:

Pros

- The product or service is functioning as it should before you try to sell it.
- Customers should be happier once they purchase as they aren't part of a pilot project and invest in proven products.
- There are relatively few, if any, risks that could negatively impact the customer, their business, or their finances.

Cons

- A significant amount of capital is necessary to develop software before knowing if anyone is interested in what you must sell.

- If there are already competitors in the marketplace, you'll have to invest significantly (advertising, price discounts, etc.) to capture market share.
- Break-even becomes a significant milestone rather than profitability.

Benefits of Transitioning to an Unstoppable Sales Machine

When it comes to selling, an Unstoppable Sales Machine can help you validate interest in a product or service before you even begin developing or producing it. Moreover, your sales machine can remove much of the grunt work from doing market research or product validation testing to confirm the market accepts what you have to offer.

To transition away from the *Build It and They Will Come* approach to selling, you need to place marketing and sales at the forefront of any discussions or decisions around product development. Validating sales and market adoption is at the forefront of an Unstoppable Sales Machine. They support organizations who want to avoid the risks of selling something that is yet unproven in the market.

Approach #2: "Sell! Sell! Sell!" Sales Approach

When I sold cars, working on the Saturday of a long weekend was the worst. We would spend time Friday night re-arranging the vehicles, adding banners, even balloons to get the attention of cottage goers who would pass by. The sales manager knew that the chances of selling a car to someone on a long weekend were slim (people were either traveling, or if they were at home, spending time car shopping was not a priority), but the dealer principal had other ideas. He would often take the Saturday of a long weekend off but always made sure to stop by and speak to everyone, including the sales manager, challenging us to get out there and sell. I recall one such Saturday it was raining, and as I sat in my office reviewing some deals I had under way, he popped his head in and asked how many calls I had made, who I had seen today, and how many cars I planned to sell that day.

The dealer was of the *"sell, sell, sell"* approach to sales. Constantly pushing his sales team, sales manager, and service manager to sell. If you had a record month, he would comment that you now had a new target to beat;

if you had a slow month, he'd pull you into his office and give you a speech about how he used to sell and his success. I never saw anyone go into his office for a meeting and walk out motivated to sell; it was typically the opposite.

Over the years, I've met various business owners, executives, and leaders of this mentality, constantly pushing their salespeople to sell. Their worth as an employee was based solely on how much they sold. The greater your sales, the better you'd be treated.

Pros

- The constant focus on sales can lead to higher sales in the near term (as employees often take drastic measures to make sales or falsify numbers for fear of being fired).
- Sales performance is often well understood as sales data like leads, pipeline health, and closes are the critical tools for managing and rewarding performance.
- Leadership remains informed of the status of all sales, both existing and potential.

Cons

- High employee turnover as employees become wary of being micro-managed.
- High customer turnover as employee turnover leads to poor experiences and concern about the organization's "culture."
- Scaling this model requires more people and increased management efforts.
- Sales fluctuate wildly on account of employee turnover and customer fluctuation.

Benefits of Transitioning to an Unstoppable Sales Machine

In the *Sell! Sell! Sell!* approach to sales, your machine will create more predictability in your sales, reducing your belief that you constantly need to push your people to sell. Moreover, moving to an Unstoppable Sales Machine takes the sales leader out of the spotlight and relies on processes, skills, and data to drive sales forward. The sales team themselves work closely together, rather than depending on the approval or prompting of the sales leader.

Transitioning away from the "*Sell! Sell! Sell!*" approach to sales can be a challenge because the owner, executive, or leader has this as their philosophy for motivating employees and achieving sales. As a result, it's often necessary to either relocate the sales leader who adopts this approach to selling or remove them altogether.

Approach #3: "Let's Wait and See" Sales Approach

The "*let's wait and see*" approach is almost the opposite of the assertive "Sell! Sell!" approach to sales. In my experience, this approach is often the sales culture in companies. The owner is not worried about increasing sales, retiring, or getting out of business altogether. It's also quite common in any company that relies on long-term contracts from their customers, like in manufacturing.

The general mindset is, "we're generating some sales, so let's not change anything, and instead wait and see if things work out." However, if a large customer cancels a contract, a key salesperson leaves, or customer order volumes drop off, these companies are in trouble. Although sales volumes might sustain for a period, invariably panic sets in when sales volumes drop, and consistently they eventually always do.

Pros

- Low focus on sales and relaxed view of how strong sales are.
- Less pressure to produce new deals regularly.
- Growth is organic and based on a few strong customer relationships.

Cons

- Sales are at the mercy of a few key customer accounts and fluctuate wildly.
- Slow periods are stressful and can lead to downsizing and even shutdowns.
- Difficulty attracting and retaining top sales talent who seek opportunities to sell.

Benefits of Transitioning to an Unstoppable Sales Machine

In a *"Let's wait and see"* environment, your machine will enable the ability to increase, sustain, or reduce sales whenever appropriate. You'll have greater control over inbound sales and avoid the significant threats posed by losing a critical customer account.

To transition to a machine, you'll need to shift the strategy around customer acquisition to be one of necessity rather than convenience. In this way, your sales machine will help you move forward consistently, expanding your reach, your leads, and your sales opportunities. As a result, you can broaden potential customer relationships without worrying about sufficient capacity, lengthening the sales cycle, and allowing for more time to create strong relationships with new customers, preparing for capacity changes when and if required.

Approach #4: "Technology Centric" Sales Model

In the *"Technology centric"* approach, the culture is often that of automating all sales using technology, often without understanding much about customers, their needs when it comes to sales, and so on. The objective is to create a hands-off sales system that doesn't require people to sell. Although they can avoid having salespeople at the front end of the process, the way they do so is by investing heavily into advertising and filling the back end of the sales pipeline with customer service representatives, who attempt to address customer concerns, questions, and complaints.

This model can be effective for selling low-value or highly unique products or services; however, it is ineffective in selling big-ticket items, which require some level of human interaction to build trust before investing.

In 2011, healthkart.com was formed, an ecommerce company providing healthcare and nutritional products. In 2014, according to founder, Prashant Tandon, the company made the decision to begin opening retail stores, allowing them to create a better experience for consumers, and to support their vision of being both credible and authentic (https://economictimes. indiatimes.com/healthkart-coms-healthkartfit-online-health-nutrition-product-website-expanding-stores/articleshow/25636314.cms?from=mdr).

Pros

- Reduced reliance on salespeople, thereby reducing hiring and retention challenges.
- You can scale it quickly and easily.
- Works effectively with low-value or unique offerings.

Cons

- Constantly introducing new technology—creating clunky, piecemeal systems that don't work effectively together.
- Don't recognize the value in salespeople—want to hand everything over to technology wizards.
- As a result of this, can't attract and retain top sales talent.
- The intention is to create an automated, scalable sales system—but can rarely break even.

Benefits of Transitioning to an Unstoppable Sales Machine

Technology is a crucial component of your Unstoppable Sales Machine; however, it is not the only component. Technology should enable your sales rather than be the method by which you sell.

In the "*Technology centric*" approach to sales, your machine will increase the recognition of the value salespeople can bring in growing and sustainably scaling sales. As a result, customer satisfaction and retention will dramatically increase, and brand reputation will grow.

Approach #5: "Micro-Managing" Sales Model

A couple of years ago, I worked with a small sales team. The sales manager was selling, leaving little time remaining to support his sales team, customer service, and engineering. Unfortunately, his varied activities meant that he was typically quite busy and couldn't always foresee sales slowdowns coming. In some cases, it was a slowdown in outbound quoting; other times, it was a large customer cutting back. The one person who did notice this was the CEO, and he was sure to jump in to try to "help immediately." His consistent attempts at being involved in what was happening in the sales department left employees confused about what discussions they should involve him in. The sales manager felt deflated, believing the CEO didn't trust his judgment.

I call this the *"micro-managing"* approach to sales. The CEO, executive, or business owner turns over all powers related to sales to their Vice President or Manager of Sales, but as soon as things aren't going as they expect, they jump in and take over. It's akin to someone teaching you how to drive and then grabbing the wheel from your hand when they aren't happy with how you are going. No one learns, and frustration mounts from both sides.

Pros

- Senior leadership monitor sales closely, watching for any unexpected changes.
- Slowdowns or changes in sales lead to an "all-hands-on-deck" approach to stabilizing.
- Sales leaders learn through observing how their boss handles challenging situations.

Cons

- The approach is demotivating to sales leaders who prefer to learn by doing rather than observing.
- It is confusing for employees who aren't sure who their manager is.
- A very tactical approach to sales, often limiting the ability to scale and grow as senior leadership can't let go of the reins.

Benefits of Transitioning to an Unstoppable Sales Machine

Senior leadership needs to stay apprised of sales and the ebbs and flows that invariably can come. A micro-managing approach limits the extent to which a company can grow, often held back by the partially informed executive who considers sales just another fire to fight.

In a "micro-managing" approach to sales, introducing a sales machine will provide consistent sales growth, and as a result, lessen the extent to which any leader needs to jump in to push for new sales.

As you can tell, each of these models has more drawbacks than benefits. Moreover, many are not sustainable and can limit the ability of an organization to increase its sales. These approaches create unpredictability in sales, and most can make it challenging to attract and retain top sales talent.

An Unstoppable Sales Machine does just the opposite. It empowers sales professionals to make sales, satisfies executives and the board in seeing consistent sales growth, and alleviates the need for sales leaders to constantly monitor, push, and worry about finding new sales.

THE NEW AGE OF SELLING: TEST, IMPROVE, SCALE MODEL

As I discussed in earlier chapters, none of these models consider the consistent evolution of today's customers. Specifically, today's buyers want to be informed, not sold; they want someone to guide them through the buying process rather than attempt to sell them on a solution. They're intelligent, educated, and informed, and as time progresses, they are less and less willing to engage in what was once considered standard sales practices.

You see, an Unstoppable Sales Machine is one in which there are three key steps, namely:

Test: Identify what works to sell to ideal customers, then repeat. The best sales professionals always test out variations of their materials and approach to determine what works well. You need to take this same approach with each aspect of your machine. Don't assume (you know what that makes you and me); instead test, validate, and adjust, which leads us to step two.

Improve: Consistently identify how to improve and adjust what works to keep up with the evolving needs of today's buyers. When we test and validate, we are in the best possible position to make changes. I'll be the first to tell you, don't get married to your process or approach; instead, continuously improve what you are doing based on feedback from testing. By adopting this approach you'll be fine-tuning your Unstoppable Sales Machine until it purrs like a kitten.

Scale: Make practices repeatable and scalable such that you don't need to hire more sales professionals to increase your sales dramatically. The best way to scale growth is to develop proven and repeatable processes and training that allow you to continuously add more resources.

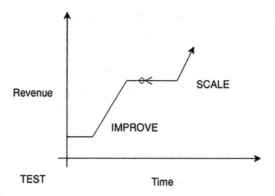

FIGURE 4.2
Test, Improve, Scale Model.

In Figure 4.2 you'll note how a Test, Improve, Scale Model approach to sales can provide significant benefits.

This approach to sales is one that provides the following benefits:

- We can test the market with new products before investing significant time or money in development.
- There is a consistent focus on selling, but not at the expense of pushing a sales team, which is often more sensitive to their performance than others.
- There are no peaks and valleys in sales that lead to a microscopic focus on the people and processes when sales are slow.
- There is sufficient incentive to continuously increase sales, as growth can be dialed in and adjusted based on existing capacity and constraints.
- You can scale without hiring more staff and without the growing pains typically associated with increasing sales.

USE YOUR SALES MACHINE TO ATTRACT (AND RETAIN) TOP SALES TALENT

The old saying goes that no one leaves a job; they leave their boss. If you disagree, pick up a copy of *The 7 Hidden Reasons an Employee Leaves*[12] by Leigh Branham before you jump to this conclusion.

I had a few careers before becoming a consultant and speaker in 2009. In virtually every instance, except one, I left because of the reasons Leigh discusses (in that one situation, I was moving back to my hometown to marry my wife, Julie—a good move on my part, by the way!).

In my work coaching and training sales professionals, many share with me their frustrations with their boss, senior leadership, the company culture, and in some instances, the lack of support or understanding they receive. Unfortunately, it happens a lot and is all too preventable in most cases. If you'd like to explore this at length, pick up a copy of my book *The Unstoppable Organization*, in which I provide the foundation for building a solid team and strong organization.

My point is simple.

Finding an employee who can get up to speed and help you sell more products or services is near impossible in today's job market, with unemployment rates hovering in the 5% range. Moreover, a recent forecast by Trading Economics[12] suggests that the labor market will only grow tighter in the coming years, so any opportunity to find, hire, and retain sales professionals will only become more complex.

Your machine will not only reduce your need to hire more sales staff, but it will allow you to empower the sales team you do have, which in turn will provide them with a greater incentive to stick with you. It is a win-win scenario.

All right, we've spent time discussing all the reasons why you need an Unstoppable Sales Machine. Now let's jump into exactly what introducing your very own sales machine entails.

See you on the next page.

Part 2

Ingredients for Building Your Unstoppable Sales Machine
Where to Begin

As our buyers have become more complex and demanding, it makes sense that we need to develop a more predictable and sustainable means to sell. A machine of sorts that combines proven tools, resources, and functions in a way that ensures we meet buyers where they are and engage when they are ready, providing them unparalleled value along their journey. Building an Unstoppable Sales Machine is what will differentiate you from your competition and help you continue to sell despite changing market conditions and buyer preferences.

DOI: 10.4324/9781003252641-7

5

Building Your Machine: The Best Place to Start

With an understanding of why you need to build an Unstoppable Sales Machine, let's discuss how you can go about building one for your company.

A STRATEGY TO ACCELERATE SALES GROWTH

Before we dive into building your machine, let's first discuss something that's fundamental to the success of your sales machine, and to growing your sales in general: your Sales Growth Strategy or SGS for short. You wouldn't start building a house without first designing a floorplan, so we shouldn't begin constructing your Unstoppable Sales Machine without getting clear on your sales growth objectives.

I recognize you're eager to get started and investing time in formulating a SGS might seem like a distraction from building your machine but let me reassure you it's fundamental to your sales success. How else will you know where to invest your time or resources, if you aren't first clear on your sales objectives?

If you've ever seen the movie *Moneyball*,[13] starring Brad Pitt, you'll recall when Brad (who plays the role of Oakland Athletics baseball team general manager Billy Beane) first meets Peter Brand, played by Jonah Hill.

Their first meeting is while Billy is trying to negotiate a player trade with Mark Shapiro. Billy is intrigued by this young man who seems to have Mark's attention (and ear) in the room. At one point, Billy asks his colleague, "who's the kid," but doesn't receive a straight answer.

By the end of the scene, not only does Billy get a player via trade, but he also gets Peter Brand to join him in the front office of the Oakland A's. In

DOI: 10.4324/9781003252641-8

the scenes, Billy eliminates his player scouts and re-builds his entire team. His analytical and evidence-based approach to selecting players is based on their average on-base percentage, rather than more common measures like home runs and RBIs.

The evidence-based selection of players based on their average on-base percentage was counter to what the entire industry was doing at the time; however, that year, the Oakland A's had a 20 game winning streak, the longest winning streak in American League history.

Selling isn't about winning a championship; rather it's about creating consistent wins that are repeatable and replicable. The theme behind *Moneyball* (based on a true story) is that long-term, predictable success comes from using an evidence-based approach rather than just using instinct.

That's the same approach to take in building your Unstoppable Sales Machine. It isn't about a simple push of a button, but instead building repeatable and replicable systems and processes that allow you to sell more, long term.

To begin with, you'll recall in Chapter 4 we touched briefly on WHY you want to build your very own Unstoppable Sales Machine. Let's revisit this as our starting point. Which of these three situations is most relevant to where you are in your sales today?

1. You're launching a new business and need to scale sales quickly.
2. Your sales have plateaued; you want to accelerate sales to levels not seen previously.
3. You find it difficult to attract top sales talent and need to introduce more automation.

With clarity around where your sales are today, let's now set some clear objectives for your Unstoppable Sales Strategy. Typically, this is something I work through with clients in a one-day VIP workshop; however, for the purposes of getting your sales growth strategy set, let's work through the steps here, together. Grab a piece of paper or your laptop, then review and respond to the following questions.

Set Your Sales Growth Strategy

1. What are your sales growth objectives?
   a. 12 months?
   b. 24 months?
   c. 36 months?

2. Where are the (most significant) changes or shifts required to achieve these objectives?
   a. Department or team structure?
   b. Sales processes?
   c. Staff capability?
   d. Staff capacity?
   e. Integration of technology?
   f. What else?
3. Considering these areas, what strengths does your organization possess that will support achieving your sales growth objectives?
4. Which of these areas possess the most significant weaknesses that are likely to hold you back from achieving your objectives?
5. Considering your responses to the previous questions, what will you need to:
   a. Start doing immediately?
   b. Stop doing immediately?
   c. Continue with on an ongoing basis?

Now that you've set some clear sales growth strategy objectives and identified what you need to stop, start, and continue doing to move forward, let's identify the key components of your Unstoppable Sales Machine that will help you bring this strategy to life.

THE EIGHT KEY COMPONENTS OF YOUR UNSTOPPABLE SALES MACHINE

Like most teenage boys, I ate a lot when I was in college (my wife says I still do). For Christmas one year, my parents, tired of feeding their son who appeared to have a bottomless pit as a stomach, bought me my very own Braun bread maker. The idea of having warm, homemade bread available anytime I wanted was exciting (I didn't get out a lot). Eager to get started, I jumped into making my first loaf. After glancing at the list of ingredients, I began compiling the flour, milk, and sugar in a bowl, poured it into the machine, and eagerly waited for my first loaf to be ready.

There was only one problem. I was so excited to start making the first loaf that I forgot to add yeast. So, wouldn't you know, my first loaf of bread ended up resembling a brick rather than a soft, warm loaf of homemade bread. Had I taken some time to review all the main ingredients, my loaf would have turned out as it should.

I can tell you from experience that the most significant risk to achieving your sales growth strategy is you. If you rush ahead and avoid setting your sales growth strategy, you'll be deploying a machine without having any clear targets. Similarly, if you have a clear SGS, but don't take your time to work through and apply each component of your Unstoppable Sales Machine, you're unlikely to meet the targets you set in your SGS. My message here is simple: take your time to work through and apply every component I lay out in this book to see the optimum results from your machine.

Enough with the banter, with your SGS now set, let's roll up our sleeves and get to work. We'll begin with reviewing the eight components of your Unstoppable Sales Machine, following which we can identify what you will need to introduce each component for your company. Keep in mind, if you don't have everything in place today, you can still move forward, but the results won't be what you expect.

COMPONENTS OF YOUR UNSTOPPABLE SALES MACHINE

As Figure 4.3 identifies, there are eight components to an Unstoppable Sales Machine.

Component #1: Funnel of Magnetism

The single greatest failure in most businesses is the lack of a proven method to continuously attract new buyers. Instead, most business owners, executives, or sales leaders take one of three different approaches to finding buyers, namely:

1. They delegate the responsibility of attracting new buyers to marketing.
2. They expect their sales team will continuously prospect to find new buyers.
3. They believe the benefit of their product or services will naturally garner the attention of buyers.

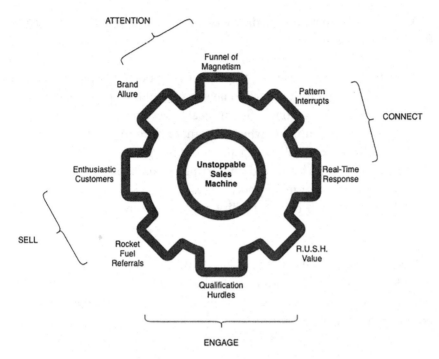

FIGURE 4.3
Components of an Unstoppable Sales Machine.

These approaches aren't wrong necessarily, but individually they are insufficient to attract the constant flow of new buyers a company needs to grow. For example:

Delegating the responsibility to attract new leads to a department outside of sales can result in sales ceasing all activities related to finding buyers, seeing it as "marketing's responsibility."

Relying on sales prospecting to find new buyers is fine, but last I checked every employee in sales needs to take a vacation and can get drawn into other priorities that take them away from prospecting.

Lastly, if you think that what you are selling is so great people will just naturally find, buy, and tell others about it, you're living in a fantasy world.

Let's be clear, collectively these activities are powerful to help you find and attract buyers, but individually they are weak or insufficient. What we need is a proven and powerful system to get the attention of our ideal buyers that doesn't take a holiday or vacation. After all, every buyer you encounter has a life cycle and won't continue to buy forever.

What we need then, is a method that continuously attracts new buyers for the following reasons:

- A steady flow of new leads that keep our opportunity pipe full.
- Create opportunities to sell to new buyers, allowing us to shed those customers who no longer fit our ideal buyer profile.
- Ability to scale up sales when we want or need to.
- An ability to control pricing and profit margins.
- Ensure our sales team (and supporting departments) remain on their toes and eager for new opportunities.
- Provide us with better stability and control over future sales and customers.

Our starting point, and the secret sauce to the power of having an Unstoppable Sales Machine, is in introducing what I call the Funnel of Magnetism, which is your proven system to attract new ideal buyers continuously. More on this in the next chapter.

Component #2: Pattern Interrupts

A study conducted on behalf of Microsoft[14] back in 2015 identified that in the 14 years prior, our attention span dropped from an average of 12 seconds to just 8 seconds. Keep in mind this is 100% of our attention, so for example, if I were to yell "Fire!" I'd only have your complete attention for a matter of seconds. There have been plenty of articles written to dispute this study; however, dispute this as some may, the reality is that the advancement of technology has dramatically diminished our ability to focus. If you want to test this theory, let me ask you, how many pages of this book have you read (or listened to) before you glanced at your phone or responded to a text or email?

Considering our ability to focus is diminishing, your ability to capture and retain a buyer's attention, long enough to share the value your product or service can provide them, is also declining. When was the last time you had the opportunity to have the undivided attention of your buyer for more than 60 minutes?

It's for this reason that the second component of your machine, once you have garnered your buyer's attention, is to provide them with something that interrupts their expectation and engages them.

To attract a buyer's attention is one thing, but to keep it requires an interruption that snaps them out of their routines and garners their attention and interest. We'll look at numerous successful pattern interrupt strategies to deploy to get just enough of your buyer's time to ensure they are clear on the value your product or service can offer them.

Component #3: Real-Time Responsiveness

When was the last time you attempted to reach a company with a question and were successful in connecting with someone (who knew what they were talking about)? If you reach out via an online chat, the first message you're likely to receive is *"no one is available right now."* If you attempt to call a customer service or sales number, you're likely to be directed into a voice mail system that tells you to be patient because *"call volumes are higher than normal."*

Let's take a quick look at an example.

I've been a long-time user of Dropbox, and the software works very well for my purposes. However, one day I received an invitation to upgrade my account for more space at a discount over my current price. Like most users, I seized the opportunity and clicked to update my account. However, little did I know that this was a prompt to a different email address I periodically use. Hence, my Dropbox folder that contained all my files suddenly disappeared, replaced by an entirely new account (tied to this alternate email address).

Panic set in. Where were all my files?

After some research, I quickly realized what had happened. Someone had shared Dropbox files with me but had used an email address not registered to my account. As a result, Dropbox (believing this was a new customer) started sending marketing messages to gain me as a paying customer. In the end, it's my fault for not looking closer at the email address they were using.

Once I realized the issue, I thought it would be a simple fix. Just contact Dropbox, explain the problem, and have them close this new account.

What I thought would be a simple fix turned into two weeks of effort on my part and hours of work. You see, Dropbox doesn't have an easy method to connect with someone to answer questions unless you have a premium account. There is a chat option; however, there was no one available when I attempted to reach someone. The only option then was to search through pages of questions and answers in their online forum, trying to find a resolution to my problem.

The entire experience was frustrating.

We've already discussed how today's buyers give sales so little of their time; the last thing you want to do is miss the opportunity to connect when they are ready to engage. For this reason, the third component in your Unstoppable Sales Machine is enabling a Real-Time Responsiveness. Think of this as your secret weapon to setting yourself apart from your competition when it comes to engaging with your buyers. You want to be there and ready to respond when your buyer reaches out.

Component #4: R.U.S.H. Value Model

When you consider how much time today's buyers spend researching solutions *before* they ever engage with sales, the obvious question becomes how to engage with them while they are doing their research.

The answer is by providing VALUE.

According to the Merriam-Webster dictionary, the definition of value is *"relative worth, utility or importance."*[15] With this in mind, what a buyer values can differ depending on where they are in their buyer journey. For this reason, we need to look at the value at each of the five stages along their journey to define what we might offer to gain attention, interest, and engagement (see Figure 5.1).

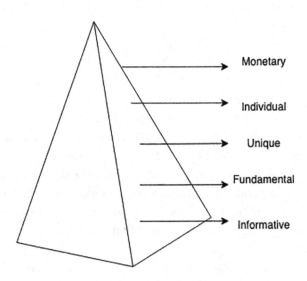

FIGURE 5.1
Five Levels of Buyer Value.

The goal of our Unstoppable Sales Machine is to provide value for your buyer at each level of this pyramid, based on their needs and expectations. The more value you can provide, the faster you'll engage your buyer and move them toward the close.

If you doubt that value can have that significant of an impact on a buyer or that it can be a differentiator in your market, think again.

How can Starbucks, for example, offer a cup of coffee at a price that is at least double or triple that of its closest competitors? Simply, they provide value to their buyers.

More specifically, the value that Starbucks offers over its competitors includes:

- The unique experience they provide.
- The atmosphere they offer.
- The wide variety of product options that allows their buyers to customize.
- Their unique branding (I still can't figure out why a "tall americano" is small).
- Unique benefits of being a Starbucks customer (i.e., Starbucks rewards).

You might look at this list and say, "okay, Shawn, but some of these features are the same as Starbucks competitors offer." Yes, but the value is something you stack, and the more you can add that is helpful, relevant, and useful to your buyer, the better chance you'll have to stand out. Although Starbucks rewards might be "competitive value," the atmosphere they offer is "unique" in their market.

We'll discuss this further in the following chapters, but for now, just know that your ability to build your machine relies on your ability to uncover and present what your buyers value most.

Component #5: Qualification Hurdles

I was never great at running track in high school, but I did okay at the hurdles. The reason was, I wasn't the fastest kid at school, but to compete (and win!) at the hurdles, you didn't want or need to be the fastest. Instead, winning at the hurdles was all about timing and balance. Picking the right speed ensured you cleared each hurdle and positioned yourself during the landing to get a pre-calculated number of steps in before the next hurdle. Those who could get their timing and balance right were the most likely to make it to the end in record time and without knocking a hurdle over.

Like the hurdles, the priority when developing new sales opportunities is not how quickly you can connect with buyers to generate new leads but the quality of your leads.

Your success depends on five factors:

1. Understanding who your ideal buyer is.
2. Your ability to find and connect with these ideal buyers.
3. How well you engage the buyer when you do connect.
4. The degree to which the buyer finds value in the connection.
5. Where the buyer is in their journey when you connect.

For this reason, spending an equal amount of time on every inquiry or lead that comes your way is ludicrous. Instead, we need to be hyper-focused on spending time with our ideal buyers.

To do so, we need to introduce what I refer to as Qualification Hurdles. Each buyer must pass through these stages in the buying process to reach the next level. With Hurdles in place, you can place your most important resource (your time) on the customers who stand out and match your ideal buyer criteria.

We'll discuss the specifics of each Hurdle in the coming chapters, but for now, Figure 5.2 represents an overview of the Qualification Hurdle process we'll be introducing.

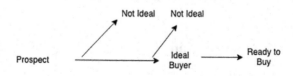

FIGURE 5.2
Qualification Hurdles.

Component #6: Rocket Fuel Referrals

It's common knowledge that referrals are the fastest way to generate new sales. However, what isn't so common is the successful solicitation of referrals repeatedly. In my experience, it's not that most sales professionals don't ask for referrals, but when they don't ask correctly, they don't get referrals, which eventually means they stop asking.

For this reason, you need a proven system for soliciting referrals. What's even more critical than a referral system is the quality of referrals you obtain. I help clients introduce what I refer to as Rocket Fuel Referrals (or RFR for short) as the best method to ensure our machine capitalizes on every buyer relationship we develop.

The steps in the RFR strategy, as identified in Figure 5.3, are as follows:

1. Confirm the four degrees of referrals for your company.
2. Identify your gold mine referral sources with proper measures.
3. Follow up mechanisms to ensure referral opportunities aren't lost.
4. Use referral expansion strategies to expand your referral network.

Component #7: Enthusiastic Customers

Aside from referrals, your existing customers are your shortest and easiest route to generating new sales. Unfortunately, too many companies tend to ignore their current customers, dismissing them as a source of new business aside from the odd referral.

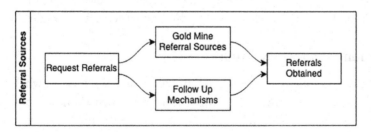

FIGURE 5.3
Rocket Fuel Referral Strategy.

That's the wrong mindset.

Instead of thinking, "I already have their business," you should be thinking, "how can I get more business from my current clients or customers?" Here are a few examples of how you can capture more business from your current clients or customers:

10 Ways to Gain More Business from Enthusiastic Clients or Customers

1. Obtain written or verbal recommendations.
2. Request video testimonials.
3. Obtain case studies that you can share with new buyers.
4. Gain introductions to their trade associations.
5. Introduce you to their peer networks or professional groups.
6. Suggest they help you find opportunities to speak at relevant conferences or events.
7. Share their favorable experiences with your company across their social networks.
8. Collaborate with you on a presentation or article.
9. Send your marketing materials to their network.
10. Recommend professional networks for you to join and gain access to more buyers.

In addition to these opportunities, your buyers have needs that evolve and change daily. When you align these evolutions with your company's ever-expanding services and capabilities, there are always new opportunities to work together!

When you introduce unstoppable selling, you need to consistently connect with, educate, and add value to your existing client or customer base. Therefore, it is one of the critical mechanisms by which you'll generate new sales.

Component #8: Brand Allure

The last component in your Unstoppable Sales Machine is what I call Brand Allure. So many companies attempt to start their journey here, hiring a marketing firm to find them new buyers, when it's the last thing they should do. After all, if you have no presence or systems to capitalize on leads, working on promoting your brand is a complete waste of time.

Until this point, we've discussed the following:

- Who is your ideal buyer that your sales team should be pursuing?
- Methods to interrupt and gain the buyer's attention.
- What your ideal buyers would gain value from during an interaction.
- The best strategies we might use to offer this value.
- How to ensure we only invest our time with buyers who match our ideal buyer profile.

After all, you don't want to attract just any client, but rather more of your ideal clients.

You won't effectively create brand allure until you have the rest of your machine up and running.

The components of Brand Allure include the following:

1. Ecstatic customers.
2. Methods to solicit customer feedback and testimonials.
3. Methods to share select customer feedback broadly.
4. Repeatable processes to automate collection and distribution of feedback.
5. Consistent marketing resource development and launch.

With the rest of your machine fully operational and under way, you are in the best possible position to introduce Brand Allure and capitalize on any investment of time or money you make in marketing. For this reason, we'll focus on the first seven components of your machine, recognizing that Brand Allure will naturally evolve as you introduce and improve the first seven components of your machine.

Before we jump into building each of these components for your machine, let's first discuss some of the potential barriers and roadblocks you'll likely encounter.

There will be some initiatives you introduce that initially won't be successful and will take time for you to prove out. For this reason, let's spend a few minutes discussing how to limit your failures and bring your machine to life quickly.

TEST YOUR ASSUMPTIONS (TO AVOID A CATASTROPHIC FAILURE)

When an airplane succumbs to a system failure that it can't recover from (despite various redundant systems), it's known as a catastrophic failure. Fortunately, in sales, we rarely encounter a catastrophic failure as in most instances, we're not dealing with life-or-death situations. There'll always be another customer and another opportunity if we seek them out. So, if you're hesitant to introduce your Unstoppable Sales Machine for fear of having a catastrophic failure in your business, relax.

Considering a catastrophic failure is unlikely, it's more likely that impatience is going to be the biggest risk to the success of your sales machine. After all, we are building a machine, which takes time, so results won't happen overnight. That's where testing and validation come into play as our main means of ensuring that what we introduce as part of our sales machine is successful (minimizing your time to experience tangible sales results).

Let's say you have an older car, and it's not running as smoothly as you'd like. It idles a bit rough and takes longer to start than when it was new. Would you keep driving the car until it breaks down or send it to the scrapyard? I'm guessing neither. What you'd most likely do is take your vehicle to a reputable mechanic and have them diagnose the specific problem.

Now, if your car is older or high mileage, the mechanic is likely to start with some basics like changing out filters and sparkplugs. Quite possibly, they'll be able to diagnose an issue right away, such as the need to replace your battery. The point is, they'll make some minor changes or improvements, then ask you to drive the car and let them know if the problems you were experiencing continue.

Take this same philosophy for your Unstoppable Sales Machine. In the coming chapters, we'll break down each component of your sales machine in great depth, providing you with steps to validate your existing processes (if they exist) and then introduce each element into your business. Approach the introduction of each stage of your machine with the view first of testing and validating to ensure what you launch will achieve your specific growth objectives.

Our goal is to introduce your machine and ensure it is tuned up to provide you with the fastest and best results possible. To do so, you must be willing to introduce and test to identify what provides you with the best results. Of course, you can always reach out to me directly with any questions or visit www.unstoppablesalesmachine.com for additional resources. But for now, recognize that testing and validation is the best way to customize your machine to suit your specific company, market, and sales objectives.

In summary then, the key to ensuring success with your Unstoppable Sales Machine requires you consistently apply the following:

1. Test out new methods and ideas before you introduce them. The sky's the limit!
2. Validate the effectiveness of each of your new ideas or methods.
3. Convert any effective methods into processes, policies, training, and automation.

Having discussed the importance of testing and validation to the success of your Unstoppable Sales Machine, let's take a few minutes to map out the process you'll use to build your machine while you continue to sell.

BUILDING YOUR MACHINE WHILE YOU CONTINUE TO SELL

Depending on the strength and consistency of your existing sales, how you approach introducing your Unstoppable Sales Machine will differ. For example, if you have a strong pipeline of new ideal buyers reaching out every day, you'll want to focus more on Qualification Hurdles to ensure you spend the most time with your best buyers.

Let's identify your starting point for your machine by identifying where your sales are at today using Figure 5.4 as our guide.

If you have low sales, or haven't been in your market for long, then you are **UNSURE**. At this stage you'll want to focus first on making some sales to ensure there is demand for what you are selling. Do not, I repeat do not invest significant time in developing your product or service until you know (by way of someone paying for what you have to offer) that there is

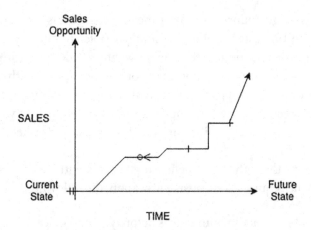

FIGURE 5.4
Unstoppable Sales Machine Starting Point.

demand. If you do this correctly, and there is demand, my guess is you'll quickly move to the EAGER quadrant.

Alternatively, if you have high sales goals but your offerings or company are new to the market, then you are **EAGER** to generate sales. In this instance, you'll want to begin with Magnetic Attraction, and continue to work through each of the steps in your machine, as I've laid them out in this book.

If you have been selling your product or service in your market for some time, but your sales goals are low, then you are **COMPLACENT**. This is often where companies reside that are either seeking to sell, or are more concerned with creating consistent operational efficiencies, rather than growing and expanding. Don't get me wrong, there may be times when remaining stable on sales goals makes sense, but it shouldn't be your raison d'etre.

If you find yourself (or your team) at this stage, you'll want to start to revisit your sales objectives, challenging yourself and your team to identify some stretch targets that both excite and scare you a bit. Following this, begin at the Real-time Value stage, validating that you are being as responsive as possible to buyers, which will speed up your conversion and improve your closing ratio. Then continue to the next stage in adding more value, to create an experience that will have buyers asking for more, continuing through the subsequent stages.

The last quadrant is our sweet spot, and my guess is it's exactly where you want to be if you're reading this book. The **UNSTOPPABLE** stage is when we have high sales goals, and have some time in your market, enough to see the opportunities that exist that haven't fully been capitalized on. In this instance you'll want to start with your Rocket Fuel Referrals, to quickly jump-start new selling opportunities, and then continue through the subsequent steps of Ecstatic Customers, Brand Allure, and then return to the top of the stages. In each stage, validate what you have implemented today, and ask yourself, how can we improve?

We'll discuss in the coming chapters each of these steps in detail, which will allow you to develop a plan to launch your machine.

_____

WHERE ARE YOUR SALES TODAY?

It's essential to validate your beliefs around where your sales are today before you start building your machine. I can't tell you how many business owners and sales executives I've met who believe they've hit a sales plateau when they in fact have a capacity problem.

Use the following guide to help you confirm which stage your sales are currently at:

1. Are your sales growing by over 5% a year?
2. Are you consistently attracting high-quality leads?
3. Is your closing ratio above 70%?
4. Are you using various software tools that enable your sales team's effectiveness?
5. Are your customers consistently providing you with certain proof referrals?
6. Do new buyers provide positive comments around how responsive your team is?
7. Do your buyers share how valuable your support has been in making a buying decision?

If you want to ensure your responses to the above are valid, contact some customers and ask them directly. There's no better way to find out if you are genuinely as good as you think you are than by asking your existing customers.

Now that we've identified the critical components of your Unstoppable Sales Machine and identified where you'd begin to introduce your device based on your business's current state, let's dive into each element in greater depth.

Let's get after it!

6

Ideal Buyers: Why You Need Them and How to Attract Them

Trying to sell "everything" to "everyone" is a formula for disaster. Instead, the success of your Unstoppable Sales Machine will rely on your ability to focus intensely on defining, developing, and then introducing mechanisms that focus on your ideal buyers. Before we go any further, if the idea of "attracting" a buyer to you is something you'd defer to marketing, then I'd ask you to avoid this tendency and read on. To be frank, marketing does have a role to play in aspects of your machine, but it's your sales team that needs to be crystal clear on who your ideal buyers are.

WHY YOU CAN'T (AND SHOULDN'T) SELL TO EVERYONE

To begin with we can't be successful if we try to sell to everyone because our time and resources are limited. By identifying who our ideal buyers are, we can be intentional about how we invest our time and money, allowing us more time to focus on those who will buy from us (because they have a need for what we offer), and less time with those who won't. Let's look at some examples of companies that recognize (and capitalize on) selling to their ideal buyers, and the influence this has on their sales and growth.

In 2019, Tesla made the decision to shift to closing its retail stores (save for some stores in high traffic regions) and moving all of the sales for their cars online. They did so because they recognized their ideal buyer was someone who was willing to purchase an electric car online.

DOI: 10.4324/9781003252641-9

At the time, buyers of Teslas were early adopters of technology and recognized the brand power of Tesla. They drive a Tesla not necessarily because they want to drive an electric car (there are other electric vehicle options they could invest in), but because they want to drive a Tesla. Knowing this, Tesla recognized that using a retail sales strategy (selling cars in-store, which has historically been how most new cars have been sold) for distribution of their cars was an expense they didn't need to bear. Additionally, Tesla knew that moving to an entirely online buying experience would reduce some of the costs associated with a retail sales strategy, ultimately helping them to reduce the selling price of their cars, which also appeals to their ideal buyer.

Back in 2000, Blockbuster had lost sight of how the behaviors of their ideal buyers were evolving. The demand for mail order DVDs and online streaming (Netflix's core business at the time) was intensifying. Blockbuster had an opportunity at the time to purchase Netflix for $50M[16] which would have helped them quickly enter this new market and continue to serve their ideal buyer's needs. At the time, the executive team at Blockbuster apparently thought doing so was a bad idea. Less than a decade later, the video giant, who once boasted nearly 9,000 stores, filed for bankruptcy. Netflix on the other hand was closely aligned with the new behaviors their ideal buyers had, and as a result, literally put Blockbuster out of business.

That's the power of having clarity around your ideal buyer. If you know who they are, and what they need, want, and expect, then you're well positioned to not only get their attention and sell to them, but remain focused on their needs as they evolve and shift over time. A lack of clarity on your ideal buyer means that any success in selling that you have is likely to be short-lived, like Blockbuster.

If you pay close attention on any given day, you'll consistently find examples of the companies you buy from, who recognize the importance of being clear on who their ideal buyer is.

My wife and I were driving through the Starbucks drive-thru the other day, and our order came to just under six dollars. We joked that the same coffee would be about three dollars less at the local Tim Hortons, which is just down the street. The discussion got me thinking, *why do we drive to Starbucks* (which is farther away from our home) to buy a coffee that we can buy elsewhere for less money?

I do enjoy the taste of Starbucks coffee more so than Tim Hortons, but that's not the only reason. Howard Schultz,[17] the individual credited with much of Starbucks' current success, knew that to capture market share in an already saturated marketplace required a clear vision of exactly who his customers were. If you were seeking an upscale coffeehouse with the finest grinds and blends prepared while you wait in a friendly atmosphere, then Starbucks was your preferred coffeehouse.

Howard knew what most don't. He knew his ideal buyer, which is precisely why he also returned to lead Starbucks through the 2008 financial crisis by closing hundreds of stores. He knew that many of the discerning buyers who invested in Starbucks coffee were likely to cut back on such expenses when times were difficult.

I can't stress the importance of being clear on who your ideal buyers are, and how this will directly impact your ability to sell (and capitalize on the power of your Unstoppable Sales Machine). Unfortunately, I speak from experience. Throughout my career in sales, I wasn't always clear on who my ideal buyers were, and it cost me dearly.

STORIES FROM THE SALES FLOOR

When I sold cars, I initially approached anyone who walked onto our parking lot because, well it was my turn (if you haven't sold cars or worked in retail sales before, typically each salesperson takes a turn with the next buyer that walks in the door). After some time, it became clear which customers were most likely to buy from me. I found that those purchasing pickup trucks were typically brand loyal, so if they were looking at a Silverado but usually drove an F150, they were likely just price shopping. I also learned that families who travel to the dealership to look at a vehicle are likely ready to buy. Of course, there were plenty of other lessons learned; however, these two tips stood out early on, and as a result, given a chance to speak to someone looking at a pickup truck versus a family that was walking through the lot, I'd approach the family.

Moreover, the more time I spent with the families, the more I learned about their specific needs, what they valued, and how I could best offer support. As a result, sales became more manageable and easier to close. I stopped taking my turn just because I was up, and instead became selective about who I would attempt to sell to, because my chances of closing a sale (and keeping the profits) were higher.

Focusing on our ideal buyer however extends beyond making it easier to close. Counterintuitively, by identifying and focusing on our ideal buyers, we gain intelligence and insights that can help us to become better at finding, converting, and closing more of these buyers in the future. We become experts in understanding their specific needs, wants, and expectations.

The lesson I learned while selling cars in my early twenties was an important one. By inadvertently identifying my ideal buyer, sales came much faster and easier. As I mentioned earlier however, pursuing your ideal buyer isn't just about how you invest your time and resources in the initial stages of your Unstoppable Sales Machine; it also helps us clarify our sales scripts and prospecting efforts.

Imagine if you walked into my office over 20 years ago to buy a Ford Mustang, and I pulled out a pamphlet on a Ford F150, sharing all its features and benefits, attempting to sell you one.

How successful do you think I'd be at closing the sale?

How can you then identify the specific pain points and corresponding value your product or service has for your buyer if you are trying to satisfy dozens of different buyers in different markets and segments?

What matters to a small business owner (cash flow) differs from what matters to a large company (EBITA). A manufacturer might care about cutting back on costs, whereas a luxury car dealership might be more prone to justify enormous expenditures that lead to a positive customer experience.

Being clear on who your ideal buyer is will make sales easier, resulting in less confusion for your buyer, and fewer questions and objections for your sales team to address.

Most importantly, it's nearly impossible to scale your sales if you try to sell to everyone as the pressure to customize and convert your product or service to suit the specific needs of each buyer is near impossible. Growing and scaling your sales requires simplifying your sales process, not adding more complexity.

To be clear, I'm not suggesting you "niche" right down to a specific type of company (i.e., manufacturers of men's oversized sandals). That would be too granular. Instead, pick an industry, or if the industry you choose is small, pick two. For example, when I first launched my business, I predominantly worked with manufacturers and engineering firms. Two very different segments, however, I had experience in growing sales in both, and many of the processes and approaches were common. As a result, I focused my language, sales process, and outreach on these two groups. If someone came along that wasn't in these segments but was interested in working with me, I didn't turn them away, but I wasn't chasing them either.

If you're still not convinced, then answer these questions (honestly) and consider each question as if all factors (availability, price, etc.) were equal:

> *Would you rather have your Ford fixed by a Ford technician or "Joe" at Joe's garage?*
>
> *Would you prefer to buy your Apple computer from a Mac Store or Sue's Laptop Emporium?*
>
> *Would you go to a specialist for your root canal or a dentist who said they could do the work?*

I'm presuming that in every one of these situations, given a choice (and where cost wasn't a factor), you'd go with the company or individual who appears to be an expert.

Let's take this a step further, shall we? Suppose you were looking to have some repairs done to your Toyota. When you searched for repair shops, there were two options. First was a local dealer who repaired "all makes and models" or there was a Toyota dealer an hour away who "specialized in keeping your Toyota looking and running like new." If price and time weren't a factor, where would you prefer to have your Toyota repaired?

Again, I'm guessing the second option. Why? Because they were specific about precisely what they deliver and how it would help you.

By identifying your ideal buyer, you remove the barriers to making more sales, and in turn you position yourself as someone who knows what your ideal buyer needs.

We've discussed at length why you need to be clear on who your ideal buyer is, so now let's jump right into how you can identify your perfect buyer.

HOW TO IDENTIFY YOUR "IDEAL BUYER"

At this point, you're likely asking yourself—"How do I find these ideal buyers you're talking about?" To begin with, let's identify who your ideal buyers *are not*. Although this might seem like a counterintuitive place to start, in my experience, it's the fastest way to sort the wheat from the chaff, as my father-in-law would say.

To eliminate those buyers who aren't ideal, use the following questions:

1. What types of customers have been the most difficult to sell to in the past?
2. What is the age of buyers you've had trouble closing?
3. What industries does your product or service not serve (or not support well)?
4. What are the titles or positions of people who want to speak with you but can't authorize a purchase?
5. In what regions or countries do you run up against the most competition for your product or service?

BUILD YOUR UNSTOPPABLE SALES MACHINE

For a more robust and printable list of questions to identify your ideal buyers, visit www.unstoppablesalesmachine.com.

Identifying who we can't sell to allows us to understand our ideal buyer. With this information in hand, let's dive in and uncover the attributes of your ideal buyer. Use the following questions to identify who you are going to pursue.

DEFINING YOUR IDEAL BUYER

Describe Your Ideal Buyer's Company.

1. What is the industry or sector of your ideal buyer?
2. Describe your perfect buyer's country, region, state, or city.
3. What is the average size of your ideal buyer's company or business?
4. How many divisions are there?
5. How many employees work there?

Who Is Your Ideal Buyer?

1. Describe the typical title or position of your ideal buyer.
2. Describe the specific demographic of your ideal buyer.
3. Identify the priorities of your ideal buyer.
4. Identify the needs of your ideal buyer.
5. Identify the wants of your ideal buyer.

Where Can You Find Your Ideal Buyer?

1. Where does your ideal buyer spend their time?
2. What events does your ideal buyer attend?
3. What does your ideal buyer read?
4. What does your ideal buyer listen to?
5. Where else does your ideal buyer contribute their time and energy?

How Does Your Ideal Buyer Prefer to Communicate?

1. Does your ideal buyer prefer email, text, or phone?
2. Does your ideal buyer prefer video or written content?
3. Can you reach your ideal buyer through direct mail?
4. Does your ideal buyer engage on social media (and if so, which platforms)?
5. How does your ideal buyer use the internet?

BUILD YOUR UNSTOPPABLE SALES MACHINE

For a downloadable copy of our Define Your Ideal Buyer exercise, visit www.unstoppablesalesmachine.com.

Congratulations! You've now flushed out precisely who it is you want (and need) to pursue as an ideal buyer. Sure, you'll have to spend some time combing through this information, something I often do with clients as part of our 1-Day Sales VIP. For now, however, you have enough information to start pursuing your ideal buyers, investing your time (and that of your sales team) in targeting the ideal buyers for your products or service.

With this information in hand, let's jump into how to get the attention of your ideal buyers, which is the key to creating your Unstoppable Sales Machine.

STRATEGIES TO ATTRACT YOUR IDEAL BUYERS

Now that you are clear on exactly who your ideal buyer is, it's time to start getting their attention.

Considering our earlier discussions around the fact that buyers today spend over 50% of their time researching *before* they ever engage with sales, ask yourself, how are your ideal buyers searching for your products or services? Of course, the answer you come up with will depend on who your ideal buyer is, but generally, most research buyers complete before engaging with sales includes the following:

Online Research Will Include

- Google
- Websites
- Directories
- E-magazines
- Social networks
- Online forums

Offline Research Will Include

- Asking business peers
- Asking business colleagues
- Contacting associations
- Books
- Magazines
- Reports

There are other sources, of course, but armed with this information, you are in the best position to determine how you can influence their research. Attracting the attention of your ideal buyers results from introducing what I call the Funnel of Magnetism (Figure 6.1). The funnel is built based on

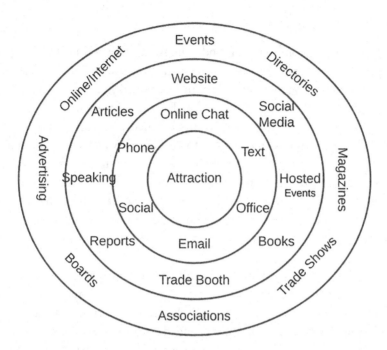

FIGURE 6.1
Funnel of Magnetism.

the information collected in the "defining stage" and combines repetitive activities, interactions, and automation that will ensure your ideal buyers come across your company while doing their research.

> Level 1—is the Attention level, where a buyer first observes your company.
> Level 2—is the Curiosity level, where a buyer first takes interest in and checks your company out.
> Level 3—is the Interest level, when a buyer first considers engaging with your company.

By contributing to each level of the funnel and slowly increasing your involvement in the activities listed, you begin to fill a funnel of leads that will act as a magnet in drawing your ideal buyers to you. Keep in mind that building out your Funnel of Magnetism requires your sales team's involvement. This is not an exercise for marketing, although there is more than likely some collaboration required between both groups; more on this later.

For now, let's look at each level in greater depth.

Level 1—Attention

Level one is what I consider the foundation. A buyer must find your company when they are seeking solutions (and in research mode). Understanding your ideal buyer allows you to ensure that your buyers find you and your sales team everywhere they seek your solutions. Let's look at an example in practice.

A manufacturer of steel components reached out while I was writing this book. Their main objective was to develop new leads and opportunities for their company; however, their sales team struggled to remain consistent with their prospecting activities. Nevertheless, we knew from their market size that there were plenty of opportunities, and we also knew that their pricing was competitive based on some market research.

We began by looking at their Funnel of Magnetism, commencing with Level 1.

My findings were that there was little to no engagement in anything related to Level 1. For example, they didn't participate in any existing online directories; they didn't belong to any relevant associations; they didn't do advertising of any kind and rarely attended relevant events or trade shows.

Actively introducing the various elements of Level 1 ensures your buyers find your company wherever they go. Once they notice you, you'll need to pique their interest, which is Level 2.

Level 2—Curiosity

Being everywhere your buyers are is a good first step, but if you blend in with the crowd, then they're unlikely to engage with you when they find you. So, at Level 2, we introduce strategies and tactics that get your buyer to sit up and take notice. For example, if you have a website that is 10 years out of date or doesn't include up-to-date information about your company or how to reach you, then a buyer is likely to move on. Instead, you need a website that speaks to your ideal buyers directly, offers valuable insights and information supporting their research, and most importantly, you need to be provocative to stand out and drive their curiosity.

The most significant gap I come across at Level 2 is the lack of current, relevant information helpful to your ideal buyers. Some examples include the following:

- A website that has out-of-date information and isn't mobile friendly.
- Social media accounts that are more inactive than they're active.

- A lack of information (i.e., reports, case studies, e-books) that informs your ideal buyer's research.
- Lack of relevant and helpful articles published in appropriate media outlets.
- Little to no participation at trade shows beyond "walking the floor."

To make your ideal buyers curious, you need to be active, not passive. Doing so provides you with three key advantages that are critical to the success of the Funnel of Magnetism:

1. You can share your ideas that strike curiosity for your ideal buyers.
2. You create the impression of being a thought leader and someone they are interested in.
3. You shorten the distance between "Observe" and "Engage" by forming relationships.

Here are some examples of this in action that you've likely experienced.

Example 1: You decide to visit a restaurant. Are you more apt to go to the restaurant with an empty parking lot or one whose parking lot is full?

Example 2: You hear someone as a guest speaker or panelist. Do you immediately see them as an expert in their field, or do they appear no different to you?

Example 3: You notice an article that discusses how to resolve a problem you're experiencing. Do you perceive the author as somewhat of an expert?

By piquing a buyer's curiosity, we progress them along our funnel, continuing the journey to the inner circle of our Funnel of Magnetism, Interest.

Level 3—Interest

Once a buyer is interested in us, our company, or our products or services, they will consider engaging (our goal). For example, they might consider emailing us a question, making a call, dropping by our office, and so on. Once they do, we can engage with a potential buyer in a discussion and start to form a relationship. However, there need to be several factors in place for a buyer to want to engage, namely:

1. We must be available when the buyer reaches out.
2. We need to be available on the platforms they prefer to engage on.
3. We need to be immediately responsive to their questions and needs.
4. We need to provide direct answers and add value during the interaction.
5. We need to have a strategy for relevant follow-up and next steps.

If you have any less than these five elements in place, the engagement will not be successful, and you'll wind up chasing potential buyers endlessly.

Think of the last time you attempted to reach a company to inquire about their products or services. How quickly did you engage with them when they put you on hold, weren't available to hire on chat, or took more than a couple of hours to reply to your email? Their priority (and the urgency with which you intended to progress the discussion) suddenly diminished.

What's crucial, then, is that when a buyer is curious and first considering engaging with us, we are ready and waiting to respond in-person and equipped with answers and value that will overwhelm them. That's the key to creating the level of attraction that will feed our Unstoppable Sales Machine.

If a buyer is even remotely confused about what you have to offer, how it will help them, or why you are the only one they need to engage with, you're heading for trouble. If you recall our earlier discussions, today's buyers spend over 50% of their time researching potential solutions to their problems *before they ever engage with sales.* I can't repeat this enough as it defines exactly why you need to introduce an Unstoppable Sales Machine. While doing research, buyers are figuring out what they need to solve their problem or help them improve, who is offering it, where their best value exists, and what they should expect resulting from their investment.

While discussing the success of MacKay CEO Forums, Dr. Nancy MacKay, Founder and Board Member, shared that her team consistently assesses what their ideal buyers'—CEOs seeking to accelerate their performance—needs are. "We need to recognize that priorities (of our buyers) consistently shift. The most difficult challenge we have is to let go of any past assumptions about what they (our buyers) need and ensure that what we offer today is relevant and valuable."

When we ensure we are relevant and valuable with what we offer our ideal buyers, we are in the best possible position to attract them.

To help you realize success I created what I like to call the Twelve Commandments of Buyer Attraction. Use these to consistently validate that you are doing the right things to be ubiquitous and attract the right buyer to your products or services.

THE TWELVE COMMANDMENTS OF BUYER ATTRACTION

1. Buyers shall always find us where they search for solutions to their problems.
2. It shall be readily evident that we understand our buyers' challenges.
3. It will be crystal clear how we help our buyers solve their problems.
4. Our offer must be clear and packed with value for our buyers.
5. There shall be ample social proof that we have helped other buyers.
6. The ways to reach us shall be evident.
7. We shall be available to communicate in real-time.
8. There will be multiple convenient methods to communicate with us.
9. We shall follow up on all communications within 1.5 hours.
10. There shall be unexpected value provided to all inquiries and buyers within 8 hours of connecting.
11. We shall present our offer to our buyer within 24 hours of initial contact.
12. We shall follow up with every buyer no less than eight times within two weeks of initial contact.

BUILD YOUR UNSTOPPABLE SALES MACHINE

For a printable version of the Twelve Commandments of Buyer Attraction and other helpful resources, visit www.unstoppablesales machine.com.

Now that we've identified how to attract your ideal buyers to your company, products, or services, let's talk about what you'll need to do to begin converting them.

7

Countdown to Conversion: Engaging with Your Ideal Buyers

Until this point, we've identified who your ideal buyers are, allowing us to target our efforts, messaging, and activities to gain their attention. As a result, you'll start to get noticed by your ideal buyers. It could be in the form of more visits to your website, more questions being fielded by your sales team, or possibly increased traffic to your exhibit booth at a trade show. We're now building a steady stream of inbound leads, but our ability to convert these inquiries into a paying customer are still delicate.

What we need to do now is give your buyers a reason to engage with interest. Remember that buyers today invest so little time with sales professionals that we need to do something that inspires them to take the next step and engage with us when they do encounter us. In this chapter, we'll walk through three critical steps to transition your buyers from curious to interested; and transition your company, its products, or services from unknown to desirable.

How, might you ask? We'll discuss the three strategies you and your sales team will need to use, starting with how to interrupt your buyers' patterns; then we'll discuss strategies for you and your sales team to connect with and convert these buyers. Lastly, we'll discuss why you need to provide exceptional value in every interaction with your buyers, what this looks like, and how to do so.

Let's get started!

DOI: 10.4324/9781003252641-10

THE KEY TO YOUR MACHINE: INTERRUPTING YOUR BUYER'S PATTERNS

We discussed in Chapter 6 the importance of introducing your Funnel of Magnetism to attract your ideal buyer's attention (if you haven't read this section, go back and do so now as it's fundamental to what we're about to discuss). Your Funnel of Magnetism will fill your pipeline with inquiries and interest from ideal buyers for your product or service, but of course this isn't enough to make a sale. After all, not all buyers will reach out at the beginning of their buying journey (i.e., when they commence their research). Some will reach out while doing their research, whereas others will reach out after speaking to your competitors; and some will even reach out after a competitor's solution failed.

Herein lies the problem.

The best time to engage a buyer is *while they are researching possible solutions*. It allows us the opportunity to convince them that our solution is the best option for them, and in doing so we eliminate any perception of the need (on behalf of the buyer) to do further research. Unfortunately, the later you connect in the buyer's journey, the more difficult it is to influence their decision as they have often developed preconceived notions about what they need, and they then measure your solution against those notions. Whether these notions are correct or not is irrelevant.

Engaging a buyer early then improves our chances of converting our buyers, and helps us avoid:

1. Price or delivery objections from our buyer.
2. Requests for additional features or value to be added (to match a competitor).
3. Delays in response while reviewing competitors' products.
4. Becoming the vendor of a commodity rather than a trusted partner.
5. Being ghosted while the buyer pursues a competitor's product or service.

So, for every one of the ideal buyers we gain the attention of, we need to stack the deck in our favor and ensure we quickly gain their interest. Not an easy task unless we introduce a pattern interrupt.

HOW TO INTRODUCE PATTERN INTERRUPTS FOR YOUR BUYERS

A pattern interrupt is precisely that; it's something that surprises, delights, and even overwhelms a buyer, creating the feeling of *"wow, if I get this much now, imagine if I was to invest money in their product or service!"* It's interrupting a buyer's expectations around what they will find and experience when they first engage with your company.

When I first flew on Porter Airlines nearly a decade ago, I did so because they offered several benefits over their competitors:

1. They had a lounge that anyone could enjoy (regardless of air miles and at no cost), filled with complimentary snacks and beverages.
2. Every Porter employee, from counter agents to flight attendants and even pilots, is always friendly and genuinely thankful for your business.
3. Porter ensures that the flight experience itself is enjoyable. Everyone on their team goes out of their way, even while in the air, to ensure you are comfortable.

For someone who flies a lot, it was a refreshing experience, and it interrupted my patterns (beliefs, ideas, perceptions) of what I had come to expect an airline could offer.

There's a restaurant close to where I live called Stevens Restaurant. It's been known for years to have excellent customer service, incredible food, and a friendly atmosphere. However, what stands out is that for every customer, there is always freshly baked garlic bread and a complimentary dish of various pickles, olives, and other rudiments. There is no charge for these and trust me when I tell you these two items alone are enough to feed a table of four. Stevens interrupts the patterns of what their patrons have come to expect from a restaurant, introducing a "new norm" for its patrons.

These are both simple examples of a pattern interrupt we experience each day in a retail environment, but what about examples of pattern interrupts in a B2B environment? Fortunately, pattern interrupts are even easier to create in these environments because they are not what most buyers have come to expect (or experience!), nor what companies tend to offer.

In B2B sales, pattern interrupts are those experiences that set us (our company, its products, or services) apart from our competition and interrupt what our buyers have come to expect. Some examples of pattern interrupts for B2B buyers can include:

- Personalized greetings in person or on the phone.
- Personalized thank-you cards following a discussion or meeting.
- Involvement of a top executive or President in customer meetings.
- A 90-minute response time to all inquiries.
- Receiving a small gift or something of value after inquiring.
- A free test drive of a service offering.
- A no-charge, no-obligation assessment with recommendations.
- A lifetime warranty (when your competitors don't offer the same).
- A complimentary product (or additional products) at no charge.
- Free installation (when your competitors don't provide the same).

The list of ideas is endless, and although these might seem overly simple for your sales team to introduce, they can be a challenge to sustain. We often become so consumed in finding buyers, closing them, and pursuing new business that we can forget to maintain the activities that provided us the opportunities to do so in the first place. It's the simple things that can set us apart from our competition and interrupt our buyers' expectations.

Case Study: Using Pattern Interrupts to Attract New Members

I worked with a member-based organization that had been experiencing a steady decline in their member base for nearly a decade. When we discussed why they believed members were leaving, the initial responses were tied to economic impacts; buyer preferences; and poor performance on the part of sales.

After interviewing several customers and assessing what the buyer attraction and conversion strategies looked like, it became evident that what this organization was providing members was essentially nothing but a promise. All the additional benefits, features, and bonuses that had once been provided such as upfront discounts on services; free assessments (for becoming a member); a signed plaque representing membership, had all disappeared. As membership had declined, the organization had cut back on expenses and no longer offered many of the benefits that were once offered to new members considering joining. This was similar to what their largest competitors were doing at the time.

We re-introduced many of the former benefits, became explicit in offering up the free assessments, discounts, and other resources for joining, and even offered a six-month free "trial run" membership. Considering what the organization had been offering in the previous years (which was next to nothing for joining), and what their largest competitors were doing, re-introducing these features acted as Pattern Interrupts for what potential members had come to expect. Within 12 months the organization had reversed their declining membership and had achieved 8% net growth.

Pattern interrupts are powerful because, as a society, we are overwhelmed with (and have often become accepting of) underwhelming experiences; some examples include:

- Make a call to a company only to be forced to leave a voice mail.
- Call a company with a question, only to be placed on hold for more than a few minutes.
- Send an email inquiry only to receive a response several days later.

We've become numb and often complacent with underwhelming experiences. High-performing sales teams and their companies recognize this and take advantage by using extraordinary experiences as a pattern interrupt to set themselves apart from their competition.

To identify what pattern interrupts your buyers would appreciate, put yourself in the shoes of your buyer and ask yourself, *"What would be unique, valuable, or interesting in my interaction with our company, its products, or services?"* Better yet, ask your existing customers the following three questions:

Questions to Uncover Pattern Interrupts

1. What one thing could we do that would make buying our product/service a no-brainer?
2. What can we deliver or offer to our buyers that our competitors aren't?
3. What is something we could offer that would make your buying decision easier?

The goal of these questions is to uncover some possible pattern interrupts that will capture your buyer's attention and make them take notice of you, your company, and its products or services.

Remember, the goal is to offer something that your buyer doesn't expect—something that interrupts their expectations. The more surprising or shocking (while maintaining a positive experience), the more influence the interrupt will have.

Might some pattern interrupts cost you money? Yes.

Will they take additional time and potentially impact product or service margins? Yes.

Do these costs pale in comparison to the powerful impact pattern interrupts can have on attracting new buyers to your business, eager and ready to engage? Absolutely.

THE NEED FOR SPEED: WHY RESPONSIVENESS IS YOUR COMPETITIVE ADVANTAGE

A pattern interrupt has the most significant impact when it is delivered quickly. In other words, speed has value. For example, McDonald's became a phenomenon back in 1955 because speed was one of the critical differentiators it offered in preparing and serving food.[18] A customer could place their order and get a consistent product that tasted good (loosely speaking), all within record time compared to other competitors. There were, of course, other distinguishing factors, but McDonald's would not have grown to the conglomerate it is today without speed.

As we discussed in earlier chapters, technology, including smartphones, Google, custom applications, and e-commerce, have created a *real-time expectation*, both in our personal and professional lives. Younger generations of buyers entering (or in) the workforce today have grown up with the experience of having everything they need literally at their fingertips. No more searching for the encyclopedia to look anything up—type it into Google, and you have your answer within seconds.

For this reason, our ideal buyers today have an expectation for responsiveness. If we aren't available when they reach out, they'll simply move on and attempt to connect with our competition.

Several years ago, we received a flyer in the mail for a Realtor in our area. We'd been receiving the handouts for a while. Each usually arrived in the mail with something unique that caught our attention (pattern interrupt), ranging from recipes, tips for home staging, to stats on the local real estate market. When we decided to sell our home, he immediately came to mind, and I reached out, leaving a message on a Saturday afternoon.

At the same time, I reached out to a few other Realtors our friends had recommended. One of the other two Realtors, whom I had never received any information from, called me back within an hour and stopped by later that day. Within three hours of my reaching out, she was in our home sharing tips and strategies to increase the value of our home for resale, asking nothing in return.

Monday morning, I heard back from the gentleman I had initially called, who had continuously mailed us information and tips. He apologized for the delay but explained that he had been out of the cell area on a family vacation. We met, heard what he had to say, but in the end, my wife and I decided to go with the Realtor who had responded so quickly and met with us that very day. Why? We knew that if she were that responsive to our inquiry, she'd be just as responsive when we were working with her, and I can confirm she was. Responsiveness was her competitive advantage, and it was the differentiator in a very crowded market.

To say that buyers today prefer a rapid response to their questions and inquiries over a delayed response would be an understatement. As mentioned earlier, most buyers today are overwhelmed with underwhelming response times. Their queries and questions are met with automated chatbots (which are useless, in my opinion, and only serve to frustrate those who engage with them), 48-hour response times to their email inquiries, and waiting for days after leaving a voice message for a response to their simple question. It's no wonder that today's buyers devote so little time to engaging with sales professionals. They've become accustomed to being put off, and as a result, delay interactions with sales until they need to do so.

What this means is that *if you can be responsive with your ideal buyers, you immediately gain a competitive advantage.* Responsiveness, that is, your ability to respond to and engage with a buyer WHILE they are doing their research and BEFORE they had planned to engage with sales, is a competitive advantage, plain and simple.

BENEFITS TO BEING RESPONSIVE TO YOUR BUYERS

- You can directly influence the buyer's research.
- You can educate the buyer on why your product or service is their best choice.
- You can identify any potential objections and counter them during an initial presentation.
- You reaffirm in the buyer's mind the service levels they should expect if they engage with you.
- You beat your competition to the sale who are not treating buyer inquiries as a priority.

When I was searching to upgrade my MacBook Pro, I (like many) searched the Apple website to look at the latest model. I had always wondered if I needed all the features the latest MacBook Pro offered, so I attempted to compare it to the MacBook Air. The comparison didn't really help much, as the technical jargon didn't really answer my question.

I reached out to a local Apple licensed dealer (not an Apple store) with some questions. He answered the phone when I called, and asked me a few questions about how specifically I used my laptop. He quickly advised that my most economical option based on my usage would be to go with a MacBook Air. He confirmed his price that included transferring my old files over and scrubbing my old MacBook Pro clean for my wife to use. His price was identical to what I was going to pay Apple for the same laptop, but I would have to do the file transfer and scrubbing myself. You can likely guess which direction I went.

The Apple dealer created a pattern interrupt from what I had come to expect in purchasing several previous laptops from Apple online. He answered the phone, responded to my questions quickly, gave a price within seconds, and offered to help me get set up and running immediately, and all at no additional charge. His responsiveness, coupled with a pattern interrupt of the additional service and support at no cost, made my buying decision easy. For the results of his efforts, he gained a new lifelong customer, all at the cost of answering his phone.

Take a moment to consider how responsive you are to your buyers today:

- How are customers likely researching to find your product or service? Online? Offline? Both?
- When they find your company, products, or services, is someone waiting to engage with them and answer their questions?
- Do they receive an immediate response that answers their question if they send an inquiry?

Responsiveness is a competitive advantage. If you're not responsive when a buyer reaches out to engage, you'll miss the opportunity to make a sale. Wayne Gretzky once said: "*You miss 100% of the shots you don't take.*" I'd suggest that if you aren't responsive, you'll miss 100% of the sales you could have had.

STOKE THE FIRE: ADDING VALUE WHERE YOUR COMPETITORS DON'T

To this point, we've discussed the importance of interrupting your buyers' patterns and being responsive when they reach out, but what we haven't yet discussed is precisely how all of this can lead to converting your ideal buyers to paying customers. The answer is that you convert by adding value. Despite all the research, price comparison, and window shopping that today's buyers might engage in, what convinces them to commit and then to buy is when their perception of value outweighs price.

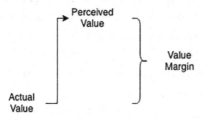

FIGURE 7.1
Value Margin.

The key, however, is that the value they receive must meet the following criteria:

- It must be helpful and relevant (not fluffy and cheap).
- It must be unique and not something your buyer gets anywhere else.
- It must complement whatever it is they are considering buying.
- It should cost nothing and not require additional effort for them to consume or use.
- It distinguishes your company, products, or services from the competition.
- It shouldn't appear readily available to just anyone—therefore perceived as unique.

Let's look at an example.

Several months ago, while grabbing a coffee at our local Starbucks, I noticed a giant collage of photos on the drive-up window. Above the collage was a handmade sign that said, "Dog of the Month." There were dozens of dogs on the collage, each consuming a whip cream beverage that I later found out is referred to as a Starbucks Puppuccino. Although I visit the location typically once each week, I had never noticed this type of sign before, and wasn't aware that a Puppuccino even existed.

The philosophy of offering a Puppuccino was one that Starbucks created, as they recognize that a segment of their customers has a very close relationship with their dogs, often brought along for the ride as their owners pick up a coffee. By offering these patrons a tasty treat for their dogs (at no charge, by the way), Starbucks attracts more travelers to visit their drive-thru instead of heading down the road to their closest competition. The Puppuccino is on a "secret menu" and not made available to the public, although staff will often offer one to customers who have a dog in the car with them. Thus, the Puppuccino adds value for dog owners and is another example of how Starbucks uses the value to attract, convert, and retain its customers.

Your goal when adding value must be to ensure every buyer your sales team interacts with walks away thinking, *"wow, if I received this much value and we haven't even invested yet, imagine the value we'll get as a customer."*

Here are some other examples of how value can support converting buyers to paying customers.

For several years I had an accountant who did an excellent job completing the books for my business. I heard from him five times each year when quarterly and annual submissions were due. His rates were reasonable, and he did good work. A colleague later introduced me to a new accountant, who, upon connecting, suggested we meet for lunch. During lunch, he offered to review my books at no charge, providing recommendations on opportunities to reduce costs or improve profits. I gladly handed over my books, and within a few days, he made several suggestions that would save thousands of dollars each year. I've used him as my accountant for the 10 years since.

STORIES FROM THE SALES FLOOR

As a car buff, I recently purchased some products from a company online, something I've done with dozens of other companies. However, what was unique about this company is that once I placed the order, I received a personal call from the company's brand ambassador thanking me for my purchase. She also sent an email with her contact information and offered to be available if I had any questions.

I can tell you in the years of buying products online, I have NEVER had someone call me to thank me for what turned out to be a $100 order, then follow up with contact information. It's amazing how quickly you can drive buyer interest and loyalty with such a simple follow up.

As you can see, value is the weapon of choice when converting buyers to paying customers. What's interesting, however, is that value is also stackable, and the more we can stack value, the faster we convert buyers.

To explain this, let's look at the five stages of buyer value and how they can work in your favor.

FIVE STAGES OF BUYER VALUE

Informative Value: Any resource that supports a buyer's research (and highlights the value of your offering).

Examples of Informative Value

- Various tools and resources
- Checklists

- Case studies
- Informative or explainer videos

When a buyer is first searching for a solution to their problem or need, does your offer help make their research easier?

Once you've provided your buyer with informative value, you'll next need to provide fundamental value.

Fundamental Value: By clearly being able to resolve the buyer's problem or by satisfying their primary need, you, in turn, provide the fundamental value a buyer expects from your product or service.

Examples of Fundamental Value

- You provide evidence that your product or service will resolve the buyer's issue(s).
- You have client or customer testimonials confirming you resolved their issues.
- You have external validation, reports, or tests that prove you can solve their problem.

As an example of fundamental value, if your buyer needs a fresh coat of paint on their building, but the only value you offer is to build them a new building, you haven't met the fundamental value need, which is a fresh coat of paint. If, on the other hand, you can offer them a fresh coat of paint, needed repairs, or the option of constructing them an entirely new building, then you've provided fundamental value.

Unique Value: This is the value you offer that sets you apart from the competition. It's through the unique value we begin to shift our buyer from "could this company help me?" to "how can I best engage with this company?"

Examples of Unique Value

- A product or service that stands out in the market.
- It is a unique feature that is helpful to your buyer, and they can't find it elsewhere.
- An additional product or service that complements your existing offering.

We discussed Starbucks Puppuccino earlier, which is something Starbucks offers that's unique (as an aside, I'm aware of some Starbucks competitors offering things like tiny donuts for dogs, but no one else that I'm aware of offers a whip cream beverage).

Once a buyer has decided to engage with your company, you need to satisfy their personal needs. At this point, you've reached the next level on the value scale.

Individual Value: To make a sale, you'll need to satisfy not only the core needs of your buyer's company but also the personal needs of your buyer, otherwise known as Individual Value.

Examples of Individual Value

- Availability and rapid response to your buyer.
- An additional benefit your buyer receives upon engaging with you.
- A personal need of the buyer that you can satisfy throughout the engagement.

Note, this is not about bribing your buyer, but rather understanding their specific desires because of engaging your product or service, and in turn, satisfying this individual desire.

If you've added value in the other areas we've discussed, the last value level is monetary value.

Monetary Value: That is, creating a significant ROI for the buyer and their company. To be clear, this isn't about having a competitive price. Instead, you need to demonstrate a substantial return on investment for your buyer, and in doing so, you add value that will secure the sale.

Examples of Monetary Value

- A clear and concise return on investment calculation (that shows a significant return).
- Additional benefits that have a monetary value to the buyer.
- A rewards or bonus system allows the buyer to improve their return on investment over time.

With each level of value for our buyer identified, let's discuss when and how to deliver that value. I've created what I call the RUSH value delivery

R.U.S.H. Value Model
REQUIRED Value (before a buyer engages)
UNEXPECTED Value (when the buyer engages)
SURPRISE Value (once the buyer invests)
HIGH Value (as an ongoing customer)

FIGURE 7.2
RUSH Value Model.

model (see Figure 7.2). Considering that the entire point of adding value is to engage and convert your buyer, the value must exist throughout the buyer's journey. It must be dynamic, not static.

Required value BEFORE the buyer engages.
Unexpected value WHEN the buyer engages.
Surprise value ONCE the buyer invests.
High value as an ongoing customer.

CREATE YOUR VALUE IMPLEMENTATION PLAN

To create your value delivery plan using the RUSH model, consider the following questions:

1. What does your buyer value (reference the Pyramid of Buyer Value)?
2. What are the methods and means you are using to add value today?
3. What value is your competition adding to buyers today? How can you differentiate?
4. What new ideas do you have for adding value to your buyers?
5. How can you validate the benefits your value will provide?
6. Where can this value be introduced (reference the RUSH value model)?

If you've outlined the kind of value you can offer your buyers and the best methods to introduce and deliver that value, then you'll have locked in on a steady stream of buyers that will convert quickly and easily.

With this in place, let's discuss how you will manage this steady flow of buyers so that your highest probability buyers rise to the top of the pack for a quick close.

MANAGING THE FLOW OF BUYERS: PULL VERSUS PUSH

To this point in the chapter, we've focused intently on how to attract, engage with, and convert your ideal buyers. You might be wondering why we need to invest so much time and effort on attracting our ideal buyers, rather than just going out and hunting them down. The answer is simple: it saves our sales team's time and energy, allowing them instead to focus on where they can add the most value. When we create a steady inbound flow of our ideal buyers, we save the painful task of our sales team having to consistently search for and find buyers. Instead, they can invest their time in adding value, which speeds up conversion. Make sense?

Unfortunately, most of the prospecting I find sales professionals using today (if they are doing any at all) goes against the current. As a result, they often lose credibility in the eyes of their buyers.

I live near a mill dam, which is quite the spectacle in the spring when large schools of salmon attempt to swim upstream. Everything is smooth sailing for the fish until they reach the mill dam; they rarely ever make it up and over. They try, but the forces of rushing water against them are too great. This is akin to what I witness even top performing sales professionals doing: spending their time chasing buyers who can't buy; referral sources who won't refer; and wind up pursuing anyone that has a budget. They're fighting to get up and over the mill dam, rather than just go with the current. Your Unstoppable Sales Machine, using the steps we've described previously, will give them the current: a steady stream of ideal buyers for them to close.

Is your sales team fighting against the current? Here are some examples of prospecting against the current:

- Sales reaching out to buyers who someone else has already contacted.
- Sales reaching out to buyers previously contacted, ignoring any previous discussions.

- Sending multiple (duplicate) responses to buyer inquiries or questions.
- Sporadically offering value to buyers and not following the Buyer Value Pyramid.
- Not prioritizing time invested with buyers based on your ideal buyer profile.
- Inside sales contradict what outside sales have already recommended to a buyer.

Some of these issues arise from a lack of having the right tools or processes. In other instances, it's just laziness on the part of sales. Your Unstoppable Sales Machine will increase your prospecting effectiveness by giving you the criteria and structure you need to prospect. If you follow the steps as I've laid them out in this book, then your prospecting will be pulling buyers toward your business rather than pushing them away.

There is no need to work through spreadsheets, comb the internet for leads, or buy inaccurate lists. Instead, your sales team's efforts focus on attracting, interrupting, and adding value to convert your highest potential, ideal buyers.

8

Countdown to Launch: Fine-Tuning Your Machine before Liftoff

With your Funnel of Magnetism in place, and pattern interrupts identified that will capture your buyer's attention, you're ready to respond to buyer inquiries rapidly; and you've introduced various aspects of value that will overwhelm and overjoy your buyers, so you're now officially ready to launch. Congratulations!

The next step in your machine then is to add a few simpler steps that will have powerful results on the effectiveness of your Unstoppable Sales Machine. Specifically, we'll design some methods that will help you prioritize the leads and inquiries flowing into your business as well as install systems that will provide you an ongoing flood of referrals, and feedback that will help you improve your machine.

Think of these steps like icing on the cake. You can launch your machine without them, but why would you when they can have such a significant impact on the results?

First, to optimize your time, that of your sales team, and to position your machine to run on autopilot, you'll need to install a few filters to help you sort through all the inbound leads and inquiries. I call these tools qualification hurdles, and in this chapter, I'll explain what they are, why you need them, and then we'll dive into a step-by-step method to introduce them to prioritize your inbound leads, allowing you to ensure time, money, and resources are invested in your ideal buyers who are ready to buy, while keeping other buyers interested in future engagement.

In addition to introducing qualification hurdles, we'll discuss how to install the components for your referral vortex that will provide you a systematic means of consistently soliciting and gaining referrals to fuel your sales. Then lastly, we'll talk about installing a buyer feedback loop that will continue to feed your Funnel of Magnetism and provide insights into adjustments or changes to make with your machine.

FUEL FOR YOUR MACHINE: THE RULES TO CONNECTING WITH IDEAL BUYERS

By now, you've likely noticed that your Unstoppable Sales Machine relies on multiple collaborations including marketing, customer service, existing customers, new buyers, inside sales, outside sales, and so on. There's good reason for this. What we want to stop is the finger-pointing or blaming that often exists when leads, conversions, and sales are lackluster. This is a team effort, as any truly effective sales system requires. Furthermore, don't think for a moment that you can "hand off" responsibilities to generate ideal buyers.

When you consider your Funnel of Magnetism, for example, you might initially believe that the outer ring, which develops the ATTENTION of your ideal buyers, is solely the responsibility of marketing. After all, publishing and maintaining online directories, researching, and disseminating relevant articles all historically fall under marketing's responsibilities. If this is how you would typically approach garnering attention, you'll recall Chapter 6 where I discuss the type of collaboration that is necessary to ensure your attention gathering activities are effective. In brief then, you'll want to follow the three rules to generating qualified buyers.

THREE RULES TO CONSISTENTLY GENERATING QUALIFIED BUYERS

1. Sales and marketing align on creating attention among your ideal buyers.
2. Your most important measure is the quality (not quantity) of qualified buyers generated.
3. Efforts to generate new leads happen on a consistent basis, 24/7/365.

Now that you've begun the work to build a strong collaboration focused on attracting and engaging with your ideal buyers, let's discuss a framework within which the groups can work to ensure they consistently attract qualified buyers. I call this the **Potent Lead Generation Framework**. Here is the framework in greater detail.

POTENT LEAD GENERATION FRAMEWORK

Define collective objectives: Identify and clarify the key goals, responsibilities, and targets for all working groups involved. These are done annually and include identifying milestone events to participate in, new markets to enter, key customer targets to pursue, and so on.

Identify key communication milestones: With objectives identified, the next step is to determine what needs to be communicated, by whom, and when. For example, considering each of the collective goals you'd identified, what information should sales share with marketing and vice versa? How can information best be shared? How will each group be notified of the information being shared?

Develop a meeting regimen: With communication milestones identified, there then needs to be a regular meeting regimen that supports communication relative to progress and prompting for assistance or support. These meetings are typically done weekly and include a plan built around the collective objectives and to monitor progress.

Introduce tools and software to support success: The key to creating this collaboration between multiple working groups is sharing information from simple whiteboards to document progress to more complex software platforms to track and communicate progress around objectives. Some of the more common platforms include Slack or Teams but can consist of various other CRM or project communication platforms.

Quarterly review and refocus: There should be a quarterly review of progress against objectives, including determining if goals are on track and needed changes. The key in these quarterly review meetings is not to get into the weeds but rather to ensure that objectives are on target and issues have actions assigned.

BUILD YOUR UNSTOPPABLE SALES MACHINE

For a printable copy of the **Potent Lead Generation Framework** to use with your marketing and sales teams, visit www. unstoppablesalesmachine.com.

Once you have the Potent Lead Generation Framework in place, you'll begin to see momentum around the quality, frequency, and volume of inbound leads and prospects. Moreover, you'll reinforce the need for a team effort when it comes to generating high-quality consistent leads for your company.

As time passes, you'll find there is a need to quickly identify which buyers are "ready to buy" and which are "thinking about buying." You'll recall we discussed earlier that we can't serve and support every single buyer in the same fashion, nor should we. Not every buyer is ready to buy simultaneously, and factors such as varying priorities, budgets, and urgency of need all influence how "ready" a buyer is to buy. For this reason, we need to introduce steps that help us determine who is ready to buy now versus those that will buy later, aka Qualification Hurdles.

Trying to serve every buyer equally, particularly as the volume of inbound leads and buyers increases, is sort of like playing a game of Connect Four. In the game, the goal is to drop checkers into columns, with the first person to complete a row of the same color of checkers being the winner. The problem for both players is that as the pace of dropping checkers increases, it becomes more and more difficult to track where the next opportunity to "connect four" exists. So, in essence, you need to have a methodology to ensure you remain focused when your opponent begins dropping checkers at a faster and faster rate.

You'll also recall we've discussed using speed as a competitive advantage. If you become flooded with qualified buyers but aren't responding quickly (or correctly) to their questions or needs, there's a good chance you'll lose their business to the competition who are just waiting for the opportunity. Therefore, it would be best to have a process in place to ensure you remain focused on buyers who offer the most significant opportunities.

I call these Qualification Hurdles. Let's discuss what they are and how you can introduce them into your Unstoppable Sales Machine.

QUALIFICATION HURDLES: GETTING YOUR BUYERS TO ENGAGE WITH YOU

I mentioned earlier my success in high school competing in the hurdles. At a scrawny 5'8" and 140lbs soaking wet, I was limited in my options for playing sports. Although I wasn't the fastest kid in the hurdles, winning wasn't necessarily about speed but rather about keeping your balance. The fastest kids often tripped over a hurdle or knocked some down along the way, whereas if I kept a steady pace and set myself up for each load, I would finish without knocking any over and without a penalty as a result.

The key to sorting through (and prioritizing your time) when dealing with a flood of new buyers who are "ready to buy" is to introduce Qualification Hurdles. These are the steps a buyer must take to identify to you exactly what their priorities, needs, and timelines look like, allowing you and your team, in turn, to deal with them in a way that aligns directly with their expectations.

If, for example, you have a buyer that expects to buy your product or service quickly, they'll rise to the top as they progress through the hurdles, ensuring you or your team can give them the priority they deserve and need. Alternatively, for a buyer who is still researching your products or services, they'll emerge from your hurdles at a lower level that will again identify their needs and the best means for you to engage with them to satisfy those needs.

Think of Qualification Hurdles like a buyer metaphorically raising their hand to let you know their specific needs and in a way that allows you to serve those needs.

The Benefits to Introducing Qualification Hurdles

1. Your sales team can easily prioritize spending their time relative to buyer needs and expectations.
2. You gain increased knowledge around when your ideal buyers are ready to buy (allowing you to further improve your Funnel of Magnetism).
3. Buyers receive the level of attention and service that they expect, which means they are less likely to consider your competition.

Let's consider the typical buyer's journey in a B2B environment (Figure 8.1).

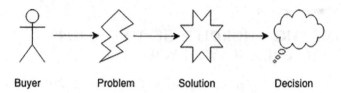

| Buyer | Problem | Solution | Decision |

FIGURE 8.1
Buyer Journey.

Setting up qualification hurdles allows us to engage with buyers at the right time, with the correct information, resources, and support to assist them through the sale.

Let's take a few minutes to discuss how you can introduce qualification hurdles as part of your Unstoppable Sales Machine. We'll start by looking at some examples of commonly used qualification hurdles that might make sense for you to use:

Qualification Hurdle Examples

- Reception who asks some specific questions of all inbound callers.
- Criteria a buyer must meet to book a discussion or demonstration.
- Internal roles such as "Pre-Sales Support" that respond to and qualify initial buyer questions.
- Live chat scripts to confirm potential buyers and next steps.
- Voice mails that direct callers based on a set of pre-designed questions.
- Chatbots with questions to direct potential buyers to the next steps.
- Websites designed with specific Calls to Action, which identify what stage your buyers are at.
- Sales scripts that identify key buyer categories and requirements.

Let's look at an example like a live chat feature. By having a chat feature on your website or social media page, you can:

- Engage with visitors to learn more about their needs.
- Recognize (through a series of questions) an ideal buyer (versus those who aren't).
- Create a path from online dialogues to in person. Examples include transitioning to a telephone or even an in-person discussion, all depending on the buyer's preferences.

Qualification Hurdles then are any tool or resource we can put into place to engage with our potential buyers; then transition them through a series of questions, steps, or clicks that tell us where they are on the scale between "thinking about buying" to "ready to buy." See Figure 8.2 for an overview of buyer decision-making.

To determine what your best Qualification Hurdles to introduce might be, ask yourself the following questions:

1. Where do we typically engage with our ideal buyers?
2. What types of questions might we ask that confirm their needs and timelines?
3. Who would be best to ask these questions? Do we need another function assigned to this?
4. How can we best position these questions to flush out high-priority buyers?
5. Would introducing automation to help with asking questions make sense?
6. What is the path that any lower priority buyer will take? How will we keep them engaged?
7. How can we test our qualification hurdles to determine the most effective ones?

For each buyer who engages with your company, whether online, via telephone, email, or in person, there must be a series of steps they take. These can be in the form of questions they answer or actions they take that

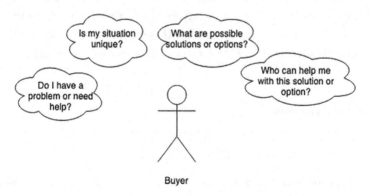

FIGURE 8.2
Buyer Decisions.

identify to us what their next steps in our sales process might be. But, most importantly, these steps will identify whether they meet our "ideal buyer" profile and where they are in their buyer journey. Remember that capturing our ideal buyers early in their journey (while they are beginning research) is key to improving our ability to convert and close.

As you consider the best Qualification Hurdles for your company, remember that a buyer's expectation of engaging with sales professionals and their companies have evolved. For example, before the pandemic of 2020, not many B2B customers believed that they would ever buy a high-value product like equipment or machinery sight unseen. Sure, they may have done this in the past when purchasing used equipment or from a supplier with whom they'd dealt before, but rarely had big-dollar purchases been purchased sight unseen. Of course, when COVID-19 hit, buyers had no choice if they needed to buy new equipment. Suppliers of high-ticket items who were smart reverted to using video and various other digital tools to enhance the buyer's research and support the buying process.

Moving forward, it's unlikely that the use of video and digital tools for selling will disappear. On the contrary, the effectiveness and success many companies have experienced in using technology to enhance their sales process offer new opportunities to reach customers who previously wouldn't have been able to view the equipment in person. Technology can also create opportunities to introduce Qualification Hurdles and better understand where buyers are in their journey, allowing your sales team to serve them in the manner they expect.

In-person meetings, lengthy dinners, and even extravagant trips can still play a role in building relationships with buyers and learning more about their needs, but fortunately buyers are increasingly willing to adopt technology as part of their journey. For this reason, Qualification Hurdles are often embraced and accepted, rather than deemed annoying.

BUYER INTELLIGENCE: MAKING YOUR MACHINE AGILE AND RESPONSIVE

Although your sales, marketing, and customer service teams are working collaboratively at this point in support of your sales growth strategy objectives, the reality is that not every initiative they introduce or method they pursue will be effective. For this reason, you need to introduce methods to collect "Buyer Intelligence." Through Buyer Intelligence, we learn how to best position our products or services to ensure they meet the needs of our ideal buyers. Additionally, we consistently gain insights on what changes or improvements are necessary to remain relevant to our buyers and capture their attention. The best performing companies in the world recognize the importance of consistently collecting intelligence from their buyers to inform how they evolve their offering, their sales, and their company.

Let's look at a few examples you're likely aware of:

Amazon started as a bookseller and is now the largest online retailer globally.

American Express began as an express mail service, now boasting over 110 million credit cards in use globally.

Play-Doh started as a cleaner that could remove coal from wallpaper, now a favorite children's toy.

What's common in each of these examples is that these companies started out selling something different than what they sell today. They used methods to collect buyer intelligence, which informed their constant evolution in the marketplace. Can you imagine if they had stuck with their initial vision for their company? Amazon would still be selling books out of a garage, American Express would be competing with the likes of FedEx and Play-Doh would be a little-known product found on the shelves of Home Depot that you would only be familiar with if you had ever attempted to remove wallpaper. It's more than likely that all three companies wouldn't be in existence today.

Your company may not be American Express or Amazon, but what are the impacts if you do not collect, buyer intelligence, analyzing it and using the information to adjust your sales process?

For starters, you'll likely never recognize if your ideal buyers begin searching for your products or services elsewhere. In addition, opportunities to expand the application of your product or service will be lost.

To put it bluntly, you absolutely must have buyer intelligence that you actually use, if you are to avoid sales coming to a grinding halt.

By this point I'm expecting you're convinced that you need to collect buyer intelligence, but you don't know where to start. Well, fortunately with the Qualification Hurdles you've now put in place, you have a tremendous amount of information available at your fingertips, if you ensure that there are means to collect the information, and you invest some time to sort and analyze it.

Let's say, for example, you decide to introduce an online chat feature on your website, engaging with visitors and attempting to move them into your sales process. Most online chat software will provide you data such as the number of visitors to your website, how many visitors engage in chat, and their typical questions.

There are numerous ways you can use this information to inform your methods to capture even more buyers:

- A trend of buyers seeking pricing information identifies an opportunity to engage in a brief presentation to inform them of various pricing options.
- Repeated questions about features that your product doesn't contain can provide insights into design changes.
- Feedback regarding exciting or useful features can inform your buyer presentations around the competitive advantages of your product or service.
- A drop in the volume of buyer engagements on chat can suggest more marketing and prospecting efforts are needed.

What can make this information even more powerful is when you also use every buyer meeting your sales team has as an opportunity to collect essential data. In other words, don't just look at the information readily available from your Qualification Hurdles but also introduce additional methods to collect buyer intelligence in your existing interactions with buyers.

Figure 8.3 is what I use with clients to help set apart what kinds of information they need to collect to inform their machine.

Being clear on what information you want to collect will inform where and how you manage that information. More importantly, it will drive the behaviors for reviewing data to evolve and improve your machine. You'll recognize changes in your buyer behaviors, shifts in buyer questions, and opportunities for changes that will facilitate even more leads, more robust engagement, and faster conversion.

The key then to the long-term success of your Unstoppable Sales Machine is in using the insights from information collected from your ideal buyers to tweak, adjust, and improve your machine continuously.

All this said, there's an additional (and compelling) benefit to collecting and analyzing customer insights and information. They provide you with ample opportunities for referrals. Sound interesting? Next then let's discuss how to create the Referral Vortex component of your Unstoppable Sales Machine.

	Exist	Stand Out	Untouchable
Intelligence for your Unstoppable Sales Machine			

FIGURE 8.3
Intelligence Gathering.

INTRODUCING YOUR REFERRAL VORTEX TO MAXIMIZE SALES THRUST

With a steady stream of new qualified buyers reaching out, and qualification hurdles in place to assist in managing how you respond to, convert, and close each buyer, you are now in the position to introduce what I refer to as your Referral Vortex.

To begin with, let's start with the obvious. The key to getting referrals is that you must ask for them.

I've found historically that many sales professionals don't ask for referrals but instead wait until their buyers offer them up. From decades of working with sales professionals and sales leaders, an overwhelming majority seem to believe that asking for referrals is somehow inconvenient for their buyers. Moreover, when they have requested a referral and not received a helpful response, they give up, often never to ask anyone again! That's ludicrous.

A Referral Vortex involves asking for referrals from literally every single buyer you engage with, whether they do business with you or not. That's right, even if a buyer doesn't buy from you, they are still a source for a referral.

Doing this alone can add 50% more sales to the bottom line!

The key to your Referral Vortex then is in the frequency with which you ask for referrals and is based on four key buyer categories:

1. **Non-buyers**: Those who engage but decide not to buy your product or service.
2. **Existing buyers**: Those who engage and (continually) invest in your product or service.
3. **Past buyers**: Customers who have already purchased your product or service.
4. **New buyers**: New customers who have recently purchased your product or service.

Every one of these four categories offers you an opportunity for a referral (or multiple referrals!). However, obtaining the referral comes when we adjust our approach and script for each specific situation.

Let's look at the specific methods to ask for a referral from each category.

Referral Steps for a Non-Buyer

1. When a buyer opts out of investing in your product or service, it's an opportunity to request a referral.
2. When the buyer identifies they've decided not to pursue your product or service, the ask should happen.
3. Asking at this stage can yield significant opportunities as buyers can often feel a small degree of guilt when informing you they are not moving forward.

Example script: *"Bob, I'm disappointed you've decided not to pursue our (product/service) and hope we can convince you otherwise in the future.*

Might I ask, is there someone you know in a similar business to yourself that might be interested in our product or service?"

Referral Steps for an Existing Buyer

1. Contact existing buyers every six months, with the premise of checking in on their experience.
2. Once you've had initial discussions, ask for several names of individuals they believe might be interested in your product or service.
3. Act on and follow up on the referral within 24 hours.

Example script: *"Susan, I wanted to check in on how we are doing? Considering things seem to be going well, we typically ask if your colleagues or peers, you know, in your industry, might be interested in our product or services. Is there an introduction you could make?"*

Referral Steps for a Past Buyer

1. Contact past buyers annually to ensure they are still happy with your product or service.
2. Update them on any new features or services you have introduced since you last spoke (make it enjoyable!).
3. Ask for a referral from their peers.

Example script: *"John, I appreciate the chance to catch up, and if you are comfortable, I'll be sure to check back in next summer. Before I go, might I ask, is there someone you'd recommend I connect with who might be interested in our (product/service)?"*

Referral Steps for a New Buyer

1. Those who have just engaged with your company.
2. Further to your company's products or services (and still excited about moving forward).
3. Make the referral request a part of the standard new customer process.

Example script: *"Jessica, I'm glad to have you join us and to hear things are progressing well. Something we ask of all of our new customers around this* *time is who else they suggest we should reach out to that might also enjoy our products or services?"*

It's important to note that in every situation, there are three keys you need to include to increase your ability to obtain the referral:

1. **Be Specific**: Be specific about the kinds of companies and people you'd like to speak to.
2. **Be Brief**: Don't drag the discussion out, but instead ask and then wait patiently for the response.
3. **Ask Frequently**: Ask at the designated times and don't procrastinate.

Figure 8.4 provides a visual representation of a Referral Vortex.

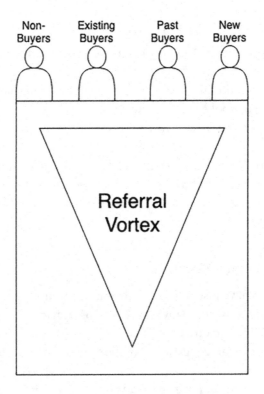

FIGURE 8.4
Referral Vortex.

BUILD YOUR UNSTOPPABLE SALES MACHINE

For a printable version of the scripts for each category, make sure you visit www.unstoppablesalesmachine.com.

Now with a systematic method in place to consistently ask every buyer you engage with for a referral, you're sure to be overwhelmed with new leads to engage with and convert. It's a good problem to have, but now we need to convert them to a paying customer. We'll discuss this next in Chapter 9.

9

Board Your Crew: Gaining Buy-In to Enable Your Sales Machine

"The secret of success is to do the common things uncommonly well."

John D. Rockefeller

Introducing your Unstoppable Sales Machine is not something you can do in isolation. As we've discussed to this point, you'll need to build a strong collaboration between sales, marketing, and customer service to make your machine hum, however it extends beyond these customer facing roles. If we truly want to create an environment of unstoppable selling, we'll need everyone on board and supporting our machine, including finance, operations, and even human resources. Think of it like competitive rowing. The team that has the greatest speed and success is the one in which everyone on the team is rowing the same direction, at the same time.

In this chapter, we'll explore the role your employees will play in the success of your machine. We'll discuss the role of leadership in getting your employees interested in supporting your Unstoppable Sales Machine, and how to gain their engagement in implementation, and why everyone in your company is in sales, even your accountant.

In my last book, *The Unstoppable Organization*, which lays out the foundation for building an organization focused on supporting your customers, I discussed how every employee is in sales. From the receptionist to the accountant, regardless of the role or title, if you aren't aligned around supporting customers, you'll never have a business that can scale and grow. If getting your team to embrace this message is something you haven't done before (or done well), and you'd like to dive deeper into the science behind doing this, make sure you check out *The Unstoppable Organization*.

DOI: 10.4324/9781003252641-12

Let's start then with a word of caution. It's been my experience that unless an employee's title includes the word "sales," many don't accept that their role supports any activities related to finding, converting, and closing sales. For this reason, interactions many employees have with your customers are treated as if they are an item on their to-do list, rather than a priority.

Changes in this mindset can and will have a significant impact on the success of your machine, and your ability to generate repeat sales and referrals.

Let's look at a common example. When accounts receivable reaches out to your customer to follow up on an outstanding invoice, what's the approach they use? Do they send a cold email, or leave a polite voice message? Do they use language that can be interpreted as a threat, or do they offer solutions and ideas to work with the customer? Here is an example of an email one of my clients received, that resulted in them pursuing a new company for the same service: *"Dear John, your invoice is now 30 days past due! Therefore, we will immediately apply a 3% monthly fee to the outstanding balance. To pay your invoice, please send a check to the below address."*

Doesn't that email make you all warm and fuzzy?

Let's be clear, I'm not suggesting that you let your customers avoid paying invoice balances that are due; however, let's be honest, haven't we all fallen behind on a payment at some point in our business? Most often it's the result of either an invoice being forgotten or delayed on account of a cashflow issue. Considering then that typically no one is delaying payment on purpose, wouldn't our inquiry be better completed as a personalized phone call that seeks to help the customer? Better yet, what if your accounts payable person offered value to your customers in the form of extended payment terms, installments, or other options to try and assist rather than make a demand? Would this have a positive impact on your customer relationship (the short answer is "yes," it would)?

WHY EVERYONE IS IN SALES, EVEN YOUR ACCOUNTANT

If you don't recognize the impact these kinds of inadvertent communications can have with your customers, just think about how much time and money was invested in attracting, converting, and closing this customer, only to have someone (who wasn't involved in or aware of the amount of time, effort, and money required to achieve this monumental task) treat them like they are a delinquent.

Until you get everyone on your team and in your company thinking and acting like an owner, recognizing that their job does play a significant role in helping to retain and obtain new customers, then you'll never truly capitalize on the power of your Unstoppable Sales Machine.

I recently interviewed Chris Crozier, Founder and CEO of C.F. Crozier & Associates Inc., who shared that he and his leadership team work hard to instill an entrepreneurial spirit in their entire staff. "*We want every employee to think and feel like an owner,*" he said.

This goal that Chris and his leadership team carry ensures their employees see customers as the lifeblood of the company that they genuinely are. To be treated with kindness, caring, and above all, the respect that they deserve.

So, let's get into exactly how you can create this kind of buyer-centric culture for your company.

When I consult with companies on engaging their team in support of their Unstoppable Sales Machine, we follow a five-step approach, as follows:

1. **Gather Attention**: We held a series of workshops to engage people from each department, helping connect various aspects of their role and serving and supporting customers.
2. **Solicit Feedback**: We interviewed key customer accounts to ascertain how to improve the customer's experience.
3. **Engage Staff**: We assigned cross-functional employees to identify how to introduce these improvements and then feed this information to the customers who offered it.
4. **Buyer-Centric Teams**: We developed ongoing "buyer-centric" teams, designed to meet monthly to discuss further opportunities to improve customer experiences and identify leads and opportunities to capture new customer accounts.
5. **Monitor Progress**: Buyer-centric teams reported to the entire organization quarterly on their progress and successes.

Of course, you and I know that everyone who works within an organization impacts your ability to attract, retain, and sell. The problem is that just telling people this isn't enough to help them embrace the idea. The only way to get everyone on board then is to have them experience the influence they can have to embrace the mindset.

The five steps listed previously are the fastest way to help your employees embrace the idea that "we are all in sales." It breaks down perceived barriers between individual roles and their connection with the customer.

Which of these steps can you introduce to create a buyer-centric, sales-focused culture in your company? Forming this alliance and mindset is the first critical step to gaining the support and buy-in necessary to launch your Unstoppable Sales Machine.

Presuming you've got your entire team onboard with your machine, the next step then is to help your employees recognize the importance of responsiveness to your buyers. We've already discussed the importance of responsiveness for your Unstoppable Sales Machine, but it's your employees who really need to embrace this fact, as they are the ones who need to be responsive to your buyer's needs. Let's dive into introducing responsiveness as a critical component of your machine and getting your employees to buy in.

ENABLING YOUR SALES: WHY YOU NEED RAPID RESPONSE FOR QUICK CONVERSION

In Gartner's research referenced earlier, you'll recall that today's B2B buyers only spend 17% of their time meeting with potential suppliers.[19] When comparing multiple suppliers, this time gets divided among the number of suppliers.

This study suggests that buyers invest less time engaging with a company relative to considering their products or services. It would make sense then that we are available and equipped with information, support, and value when a buyer reaches out.

The same Gartner study also provides a view of what the typical B2B buyer journey looks like today. To say it's complex would be an understatement.

A *Harvard Business Review* article from several years ago identified this emerging trend.[20] It suggested that the outcome of an increasingly complex buying process is that today's buyers are stressed and have difficulty making their buying decision.

When your employees are responsive to your buyers, they de-stress the buying experience, making it easy to buy from you. As a result, less stress means your buyers find it easier to buy from you, which means they'll buy faster, buy more often, and tell others. This is a behavior we want!

When we place our buyers first and have an employee culture that recognizes the impact they and their role have on the customer, employees are more open to putting customer needs ahead of everyone else.

So, let's get down to exactly how to integrate responsiveness into your buyer-facing activities.

INTEGRATING RESPONSIVENESS INTO BUYER-FACING ACTIVITIES

1. **Buyer Feedback**. Interview key buyers, potential buyers, and past buyers to understand where weaknesses in buyer-facing activities exist. Doing so provides a basis for the initial changes you'll make and eases the adoption for employees who may dispute your views.
2. **Empowered Teams**. Using your buyer-centric teams, assign areas for improvement based on feedback collected. Employees should be empowered to make decisions and recommendations and ensure they engage those in the impacted roles.
3. **Response Measures**. Introduce measures that monitor responsiveness in these areas. Examples include call wait times, email response times, voice mail response times, and so on. If a buyer has identified delays, there should be a measure to confirm the "new" response time is as expected.
4. **Metrics that Matter**. Too many measures only get lost amid other priorities. Someone should be responsible for monitoring and reporting on all actions to senior leadership and the cross-functional teams.
5. **Leadership Commitment**. With improvements and measures in place, leadership must fully support improvements based on recommendations from the buyer-centric teams. Act quickly on recommendations—no second-guessing what the team has suggested, although further discussions are encouraged.

Congratulations! You now have a structure in place that will ensure that ideas for improvements from your buyers are monitored, measured, and further improved as necessary.

Enabling your employees then to be responsive starts with introducing the right processes, tools, and culture. Let's look at each of these three areas and view some examples.

PROCEDURES THAT SUPPORT RESPONSIVENESS

Early in my career, I worked for a company that was in a highly regulated industry. Several thousand employees worked on the same site, and as a result, there were thousands of procedures. Although it was many years ago now, the count of active procedures (that employees were supposed to be aware of) was well over 2,000.

That's a lot of procedures.

I'm a fan of procedures to capture best practices and provide a training resource that guides employees. I find, however, there are three issues many companies struggle with when it comes to having procedures available for their employees to reference, namely:

1. **They have no procedures**: The risk here is that there is no way to create consistency in how your employees perform.
2. **Procedures exist but are out of date**: This is often the result of a former employee who created them in a vacuum, and as a result, they aren't current, and no one uses them.
3. **There is an overwhelming number of procedures**: This often exists in very technical or regulated industries, where repeatability is a way to reduce risk.

There are downfalls to each of these approaches to procedures; the first two are obvious. However, they should provide guidance and create consistency in how employees approach various aspects of their role. Any procedure that resides in a binder or online file isn't readily accessible, and provides absolutely no value to employees in their day-to-day activities. The risk, of course, is that, without procedures readily accessible and referenced, your buyers and customers are likely to have very different experiences, often for the same request or concern.

The opposite situation then is to have too many procedures, which can stifle creativity. When you have a plethora of procedures in place, leaders tend to become overly concerned with reinforcing standards, and employees become reliant on following them. That's good, of course, but what often happens is that the number of procedures stifles creativity. Employees, in turn, become fearful of doing anything that is not documented or captured in a procedure, and they presume (for obvious reasons) that they shouldn't challenge existing thinking.

An overabundance of procedures and policies kills innovation and creativity. Moreover, it slows down responsiveness, as employees tend to defer to what a policy or procedure says, rather than respond to what a buyer or customer wants.

To ensure an overabundance of procedures don't lock down your employees, ensure all of your buyer-facing procedures meet the following criteria:

1. The expected response time to all buyer inquiries is clear.
2. The best method to respond (based on buyer communication) is included.
3. Employees can respond and resolve buyer and customer needs without escalation.
4. Information or questions that do require escalation have a rapid process for doing so.
5. Buyer and customer response times are a key measure of success.

Considering that the procedures you introduce will aid in guiding your employees in support of your Unstoppable Sales Machine, let's now look at some resources that will enable your sales team to be more efficient, and in turn more responsive.

TOOLS THAT ENABLE BUYER RESPONSIVENESS

Periodically I conduct my Forensic Sales Audit for clients. When I do, we start by looking at the number of procedures they have in use, how often employees use those procedures related to buyer and customer interactions, and the enablement tools available to help them quickly integrate the practices into their roles. The results rapidly identify the responsiveness, consistency, and creativity buyers and customers receive.

There are six types of sales enablement tools to consider that will directly enhance your ability to respond quickly, serve, and support your buyers and customers.

SALES ENABLEMENT TOOLS THAT SUPPORT BUYER RESPONSIVENESS

1. **Customer Relationship Management (CRM)**: Most CRM software today has easily accessible dashboards that can be accessed via mobile and allows employees to quickly access information critical to ensuring a rapid (and valid) response.
2. **Sales Content Management**: One of the most significant challenges a large company can encounter is ensuring sales have access to, and use, the appropriate materials when speaking to buyers. Software such as Seismic (https://seismic.com/) offers an easy way to manage sales content, categorize it, and even limit access based on pre-set criteria—no more issues with the sales team sending the wrong presentation or materials to buyers.
3. **Coaching and Training Tools**: Software that houses easily referenced videos and scripts for all sales or buyer-facing employees is a great way to bring training to life and reinforce internal best practices. Best of all, videos can be updated regularly to remain dynamic and supportive as circumstances change. Software like Brainshark (www.brainshark.com/) offers an easily accessible platform for any buyer-facing role.
4. **Sales Engagement**: If you're looking to review and analyze buyer and customer data to determine the best products, services, or communication channels to use, then software like Outreach (www.outreach. io/) may be a good option. Whatever sales engagement software you consider, ensure it integrates with your existing CRM for more automation and information centralization opportunities.
5. **Sales Management**: If you've set procedures and expectations around response time, you'll need a way to monitor and manage these expectations. Software such as Clari (www.clari.com/) provides real-time

monitoring of KPIs in an easy-to-view dashboard. Most importantly, these tools allow for sharing information with buyer-facing roles, which is critical to gaining buy-in and support of achieving the measures by employees.

There are literally hundreds of software and other resources you can use to enable your team to be effective, efficient, and responsive to your buyers. Considering our goal is for you to quickly launch (and achieve results with) your Unstoppable Sales Machine, I've covered the basics here to get you started. The last thing we want is for you to get stuck in reviewing and selecting software, as these tools are complimentary to your machine, not fundamental.

BUILD YOUR UNSTOPPABLE SALES MACHINE

For a more robust list of sales enablement tools and software that I use with clients, visit www.unstoppablesalesmachine.com.

So, if procedures provide your buyer-facing roles a guide to follow, and you select the right enablement tools to support their application, is that all that you need?

HOW TO ENGAGE YOUR TEAM AND SELL MORE

As we've discussed to this point, the key to the success of your Unstoppable Sales Machine is to "engage" your entire team in your mission. I've had clients who want to mandate their employees support the various aspects of the sales machine; however, it never ends well. What we want is buy in, not compliance.

A few years ago, my son, about nine years old at the time, brought home some math homework he was to complete. It was straightforward multiplication and division, which he was struggling with (now he's a math wizard, go figure!). When I offered to help, I started by asking him to show me where he was struggling, and he proceeded to show me how he was attempting to calculate his answer. It was a completely different approach to calculating math than what I had learned as a kid, so after listening for a few minutes, I took the pencil and said, "let me show you how we learned math."

He quickly picked up what I showed him and headed back to school with his homework completed the next day. However, when he arrived home that evening, he was disappointed. He had the same assignment with him and said, "Dad, my teacher said I didn't do the homework correctly, so I need to redo it, and this time without your help—using the method we learned in class."

I was initially frustrated with the teacher; however, my wife, a child educator, was able to fully explain the new way to do math and shared with me why learning this new method was important.

My point is this. Even basic math involves more than one way to get to the correct answer. So, just because you spend time designing and introducing your Unstoppable Sales Machine doesn't mean you won't find ideas to improve it along the way. New ideas have a way of bringing new (or better) results. Engaging your team, rather than just telling them what to do in support of your machine, taps into their individual creativity.

When you tap into the *creativity* of your team you find new ways to continuously improve your Unstoppable Sales Machine. Let's look at some common examples my clients have encountered:

- Your sales team identifies a new source of potential leads to pursue.
- Your customer service team suggests a change in your contract language to reduce buyer frustration and contract delays.
- Your marketing team suggests a new piece of software that will make buyer-facing marketing materials more accessible for your sales team.
- Inside sales suggest a weekly meeting with outside sales to align on customer accounts.

The list of opportunities and ideas to improve your machine is endless but only relevant if you enable your employees to be creative in supporting your machine.

In addition to tapping into the creativity of our employees, when we engage them in introducing our machine we gain direct access to their unabridged feedback. After all, it's our employees, including sales, marketing, customer service, and others that engage with our buyers daily. For this reason, and to ensure we capture feedback that can assist in improving our machine, there are several additional steps you'll want to take.

1. Monthly meetings with department champion reviewing components of your machine, including what's working, what's not, and how to improve.
2. Quarterly meetings with all employees to discuss the state of your customers, business, and opportunities that exist.
3. Annual summaries of new customers captured, potential customers on the horizon, and customers lost (and reasons for such).

The more often you communicate and bring your team together, the greater the creativity you'll entice, and in turn, the more effective your sales machine will be.

Case Study: Using Team Updates to Solicit Employee Ideas and Feedback

A manufacturer I worked with who was trying to increase their sales, was struggling to get their team working together and ensure a rapid quote response for buyers. Delays in quotes were leading to lost opportunities and new buyer complaints.

Once an opportunity to quote was secured, sales were quick to forward new opportunities to the inside sales team to quote; however, it often took nearly a week for quotes to be finalized and sent to the customer. When we investigated, we learned that many of the employees responsible for constructing the quotes were being pulled into other meetings and activities that took them away from their core role.

After discussing the challenge, the sales executive introduced a daily standing meeting to review (visually on a large screen) a summary of all outstanding quotes. The meeting included inside sales, outside sales, the quote team, and engineering. During the meeting each quote was mentioned, and a commitment date for completion was identified. Additionally, any potential delays or obstacles were shared, and a resolution was determined on the spot.

Indirectly this meeting served to ensure that all the employees involved were aware of the priority and importance of various quotes and customers. If a customer was new, their quote was often prioritized above others to ensure a rapid response. Additionally, sales were notified immediately if feedback was required from the customer to complete a quote. This daily communication resulted in a reduction of quote time from an average of over five days, to under three, with no other significant changes.

When you capitalize on the ideas and recommendations your employees have, you'll not only increase their interest in the success of your Unstoppable Sales Machine, but you'll also enable them to be part of your machine. The idea of introducing your Unstoppable Sales Machine will transition from your idea to their idea. That's the key to getting your team to buy into your new Unstoppable Sales Machine.

Part 3

Prepare the Rockets
Launching Your Machine

The ability to execute and launch your machine will make the difference between selling more and dominating your market. With the components of your Unstoppable Sales Machine now identified and developed, it's time to put your machine (and your team) into action. So let the countdown to launch begin!

DOI: 10.4324/9781003252641-13

10

Launch Your Machine (Prepare for the Worst, Expect the Best)

With the components of your Unstoppable Sales Machine now in place and your team aligned and excited to support its success, you're ready to launch. In this chapter, we'll walk through the specific steps you'll need to take to launch your machine, progressing you from zero to sales hero in no time flat!

We'll start by discussing how to introduce your sales machine alongside your existing sales activities, and why it's a good idea to mirror these for six months, in some cases longer. Then we'll discuss when to begin transitioning away from old practices, specifically what you'll need to stop doing, and what you'll want to continue doing to ensure long-term sales growth. Lastly, we'll discuss some essential measures you'll want to put into place early on to monitor the success of your Unstoppable Sales Machine, allowing you to fine-tune its performance.

READY, AIM, FIRE: STEPS TO LAUNCH YOUR UNSTOPPABLE SALES MACHINE

Notice the order of the words in the title above. They don't say "Fire" then "Ready." There's a reason for this. As much as you may be excited and even relieved to have your own Unstoppable Sales Machine in place, not taking the time to follow the steps I've laid out in this book, in the order I've laid them out, is risky. I've worked with enough companies, in enough sectors, to know what works, and what doesn't.

DOI: 10.4324/9781003252641-14

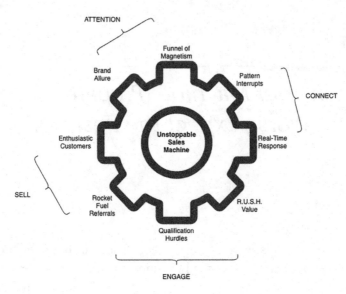

FIGURE 10.1
Unstoppable Sales Machine Components.

In Figure 10.1, I've laid out all of the components for you to introduce and launch your machine successfully.

> **BUILD YOUR UNSTOPPABLE SALES MACHINE**
>
> If you'd like a printed version of these stages to post on your wall or at your desk, visit www.unstoppablesalesmachine.com.

Let's take a few minutes then to briefly recap each stage of your machine and piece them together in a simple summary that you can use to ensure you complete all the necessary steps to launch.

STEPS TO INTRODUCING YOUR UNSTOPPABLE SALES MACHINE

1. Develop Your Sales Growth Strategy

Identify your sales growth objectives for the coming months and years. Identify in what regions and sectors you want growth, and the products or services that present the greatest opportunities to do so.

2. Develop a Plan for Introducing Each Component of Your Machine

Review each component of your machine and contrast them against your current systems or processes. Identify gaps between what you are currently doing and what you'll need to do. Then, consider how changes in processes, sales skills, and technology can support introducing each component.

3. Identify Potential Risks or Obstacles You'll Encounter

With gaps and steps identified, identify potential risks, barriers, or obstacles you're likely to encounter. Prioritize each risk by considering the likelihood it will occur and the seriousness of its impact. Figure 10.2 demonstrates how to contrast these two variables to develop priority.

4. Formulate Mitigating and Contingent Actions

For each risk, identify the actions you can take to either avoid the risk or overcome it in the event it occurs. Place more effort in the risks that are of higher priority. I call this the "plan for the worst hope for the best approach." By being prepared with clear plans to avoid or overcome risks, you lessen the likelihood they will occur, and if they do, you'll have a strategy to overcome them.

5. Identify Champions for Each Component of Your Machine

Each component of your machine should have a champion—someone with overall responsibility for its introduction and successful launch. In a smaller company, one person may be the champion for multiple areas; however, do your best to engage as many of your team members in your

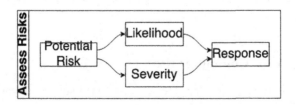

FIGURE 10.2
Assess Risks.

plans as possible (as long as they have some expertise or knowledge in the area they are championing) to drive interest and support while reducing the burden of introducing your machine all by yourself.

6. Develop Weekly Action Plans for Implementation

As you progressively begin introducing each component of your machine, set weekly targets for completion. We want to avoid getting carried away creating Gant charts and project plans for launching our machine, and instead just ensure that we have clear actions that can be measured. Breaking activities down into weekly steps will avoid them being too vague and allow you to monitor them closely to ensure they are successful.

To give you an example, introducing your Funnel of Magnetism might be broken down into steps such as:

Week 1: Identify online sources our ideal buyers frequent, including websites, forums, social media, and so on.

Week 2: Identify offline sources our ideal buyers use, including periodicals they read, events they attend, associations they belong to, and so on.

Week 3: Review current activities in both online and offline areas to identify gaps or areas we can increase or introduce activities to gain our buyers' attention.

Week 4: Prioritize activities identified in week 3 and devise a plan to introduce or improve the top five activities. Assign champions to develop work plans, weekly targets, and metrics, reporting on status each week.

Week 5: Champions to meet with their team to devise work plans, targets, and metrics. Submit their first report at the end of the week to identify what has been completed and what next steps are.

Week 6: Set a meeting with each champion to begin discussing any new technology, processes, or resources necessary to complete their work plans.

7. Develop Your Communication Protocol

As discussed in the previous chapter, the key to the success of your machine is to engage your employees. The more they know, the better chance they will pitch in to support you and help move your sales machine forward.

To this end, create a weekly communication protocol to update employees on your progress.

Examples of what you might include in your communication protocol include:

- What steps have you taken?
- What risks have you encountered?
- What actions are you taking to overcome the threats?
- Who else needs to be involved?
- What results or changes are you experiencing so far?
- What are the next steps you'll be taking?

Early discussions will be swift, likely only 10 minutes in duration; however, as you get deeper into implementation, the update may take upwards of one hour. When this becomes the case, consider breaking out communication multiple times during the week to keep meetings brief and focused on progress.

8. Monitor Each Team's Progress Closely

In my experience it's very easy for your implementation to slow or even stall. After all, if the elements you're introducing were easy, your teams would have likely introduced them already. Areas such as introducing technology to support your machine, finding and engaging staff resources to implement aspects of your machine, and even finding expertise in areas teams are unfamiliar with, can all lead to progress coming to a grinding halt. Let me share an example of how this can easily happen.

A client of mine had several employees making outbound sales calls using their existing CRM software. They had captured notes and recordings of calls, which they used to support additional calling. The process worked great, except that the project became stalled when changing their CRM to different software. Employees became stuck when trying to determine how to best transition various comments and notes from the existing CRM software to the new software.

The employees had taken the steps to identify how to bring this data over using a service the new CRM software company could offer, but it was going to cost my client thousands of dollars, which the employees knew was unreasonable. It took my client several discussions to convince the employees that existing notes could be maintained in a spreadsheet for ease of reference, and new notes could be entered in the new CRM.

Although engaging employees in the implementation of your machine is crucial to its success, they can get hung up on minor steps or areas they don't have expertise in, and it's for that reason that you'll want to remain involved and up to date with weekly check-ins to help overcome any such barriers.

9. Encourage Your Champions to Champion

It's important to identify and engage champions in the implementation of your machine, as they will be the ones to drive the implementation forward despite the impediments and obstacles that will undoubtedly arise. For this reason, be selective in who you choose, making sure you pick the right champions, those who are excited about seeing your machine come to life, and who are optimistic and able to continue pushing forward. You'll also need to provide these people with some degree of autonomy and authority to make decisions to ensure they can move forward.

10. Build a Community among Your Champions

To keep the project aligned and minimize the impacts of delays and obstacles, have champions meet weekly to discuss their progress and share ideas on overcoming issues they encounter. Historically I've found that one hour each week is more than sufficient and can be attained if you use an agenda and spread the time between each champion's report out equally. Sitting in on this meeting is also important to help you maintain oversight on your progress.

With the steps in your plan set out, champions selected, workplans and targets identified, and weekly progress reporting under way, let's dive into some specific tactics you'll need to follow to execute your plan swiftly and effectively.

EXECUTION OF YOUR PLAN: FROM PAPER TO PRACTICE

Launching your Unstoppable Sales Machine is the point at which the rubber hits the road. Those who do so separate themselves from just reading this book and having a desire for consistent and repeatable sales.

Despite your best intentions, having all the key components lined up, and the support of your team behind you, successful implementation of your Unstoppable Sales Machine will require work.

In my experience, most senior executives and sales leaders have the best intentions to support the introduction of an Unstoppable Sales Machine. Unfortunately, however, their days are already overflowing with various priorities, unexpected fires to contend with, and a wide variety of employee and customer issues. When you add other priorities and activities in support of developing your machine, without first ensuring sufficient time, focus, resources, and capacity, the implementation can tend to fall apart.

To put this into context, consider the last time you formulated a corporate strategy. Having formulated a solid strategy, you communicated it to your team, and possibly even began some regular check-in meetings to ensure its progress. Yet, 12 to 18 months later, the strategy (and any progress against it) was halted. A recent *Harvard Business Review* article[21] suggested that 67% of well-formulated strategies fail in their execution. Therefore, it behooves us to avoid falling into this same trap with the implementation of your machine.

Until this point in the book, we've discussed all the components you'll need to introduce your Unstoppable Sales Machine. We've also explored a wide variety of best practices to get your team involved, excited, and interested in helping with the implementation and adoption of new processes and methods of selling. Now let's roll up our sleeves and get to work on how to transition your plans from paper to reality.

We'll start by discussing how to transition your existing buyers (that your sales team have been engaged with already) into your machine, and doing so without scaring them away!

EASE YOUR EXISTING BUYERS INTO YOUR MACHINE

Fortunately, this is not as complex or difficult as you might think, considering your machine ensures you engage with your buyers more frequently, paying more attention to their needs and interests.

The key is to set a date upon which new buyers will enter your machine versus being susceptible to old or past practices. First, let's revisit and then consider each of the phases of your machine and the potential change required (if any):

Phase 1: Attention Phase

At this point we introduce your funnel of magnetism, various pattern interrupts, and real-time responsiveness. As you might imagine, there are no direct impacts on existing buyers during this phase other than we'll be generating more attention for your company, its products, or its services. These new steps and resources will create *more attraction* to your company and brand, so there is no need to advise or update customers or clients about these changes. These may assist in closing some of your existing buyers faster as they start to see your company everywhere they go.

Phase 2: Interest and Engage Phases

During the Interact phase, we introduce RUSH Value and Qualification Hurdles. As a result of the new hurdles existing buyers may have to traverse, there may be some confusion as to why buyers are susceptible to additional questions or steps they need to take. If, for example, an existing buyer (who has already engaged with your company) visits your website or calls your office and is now asked some questions (qualification hurdles) to direct their call, they may be confused as to why the questions are now necessary.

To avoid this confusion, you'll need to identify all your existing leads and buyers, clarify where they are in their journey, and then purposefully communicate the changes and the benefits these will provide them. Don't stress, this is easier than you might think. Also, this type of communication with your buyers will be well received and offer you another touch point to accelerate their journey toward a close.

I typically recommend you segment your buyers into three categories to educate them correctly, using the following steps for each category:

High Potential Buyers: Considering the importance of these buyers, the steps to take are much more critical to ensure you retain and convert these buyers, as follows:
1. Send a personalized note from the President or an executive of the company, advise of some new interactions they may experience,

and discuss how it will streamline their experience, providing additional value.

2. Offer to be available if there are any questions or concerns and leave a direct number and email for any responses.

3. Monitor these channels closely and respond quickly if you receive any inquiries or concerns.

Low Potential Buyers: Send an email (from the salesperson they initially connected with) with similar content to the previous message. These offer you a buyer touchpoint opportunity! Again, encourage the buyer to re-engage with their sales representative and encourage them to take the next step in their journey.

Unresponsive Buyers: Like the approach for high potential buyers, send an email from the President or an executive within the company. Use this as an opportunity to re-engage, so focus the communication on the additional value you are providing new clients or customers and request they book a meeting with their sales representative to discuss how this will be helpful to them. Again, make sure to include clear contact information.

Phase 3: Make the Sale

Creating enthusiastic customers and continuously requesting referrals are the steps in our Sell Phase. These will serve to increase our interactions with existing buyers. Considering we already have a relationship in place, there is no need to advise the buyer of any changes or updates.

It's important to mention however that when it comes to introducing your Rocket Fuel Referral process, there is an opportunity to announce the process as a new program to existing buyers. You can do this by using language that suggests you are providing them with an "opportunity" to help other companies who they decide to refer. Remember the language used in all these communications must focus on the buyer and bring them value.

Phase 4: Scale and Grow

We haven't discussed scaling up your sales using your Unstoppable Sales Machine as of yet; however, it's important to mention there are no specific impacts to existing buyers or customers during this phase, so no additional communications are required.

BUILD YOUR UNSTOPPABLE SALES MACHINE

For sample scripts you can use with customers to introduce them to the benefits and value your Unstoppable Sales Machine offers, visit www.unstoppablesalesmachine.com.

Now that we've discussed how to introduce and integrate existing buyers into your Unstoppable Sales Machine, let's discuss some pitfalls you should be aware of.

AVOIDING AND OVERCOMING COMMON PITFALLS WHEN INTRODUCING YOUR MACHINE

As we've discussed throughout this book, introducing your Unstoppable Sales Machine doesn't come without some challenges. In this section then let's discuss some pitfalls you'll want to avoid (and how you can avoid them) when introducing your machine.

First, we'll look at areas for potential failure when introducing your machine and how to avoid them.

COMMON PITFALLS TO AVOID

1. Stop Existing Selling (and Prospecting) Activities while Launching Your Machine

If you haven't laid out a clear plan for all aspects of your sales machine, instead of rushing ahead and only partially planning for critical components, then there's a good chance your machine will fail. One of the keys you'll recall I mentioned earlier is the need to continue reaching out to buyers (i.e., prospecting) as you launch your machine until you reach a point that inbound leads overwhelm leads from outreach.

Here's an example. While working with a software company to introduce their Unstoppable Sales Machine, the Vice President of Sales, eager for more sales, kept asking, *"Just tell us what we need to do, and we'll do it!"* Despite his eagerness to move forward, execution was a weakness. I had recommended, for example, that their outreach activities, and prospecting, continue; however, as we began to set up their sales machine, they eased off outreach. As you might imagine leads began to lessen and disappointment about the effectiveness of their machine set in. Think about it this way: every engine takes time to warm up. If you were just to hop in and hit the gas, you'd end up doing more damage than good. Your Unstoppable Sales Machine works the same way. You need to ease into implementing and testing to ensure you achieve top sales performance.

Considering you have methods to generate new business today, you'll need to operate them in parallel as you build your sales machine, providing you with a continued influx of business opportunities.

2. Introducing Components of Your Machine without a Plan

This book provides you with a step-by-step approach to introducing your Unstoppable Sales Machine. But, if you move forward with implementing components of your machine without setting your sales growth strategy, or following the order that I recommend, you won't achieve the level of sales possible. Don't misunderstand, adding new activities that will support generating more sales is always a good thing, but you won't achieve the level of success possible for your sales.

If you want to achieve the levels of success with your machine that are possible, use this book as your guide. After all, failure to achieve a goal is one thing; failure to have one is just negligent.

BUILD YOUR UNSTOPPABLE SALES MACHINE

To help you with implementation, I've created a workbook that you and your team can follow. For your copy, visit www.unstoppable salesmachine.com.

3. Failing to Closely Monitor Your Progress

During my early years in high school, I was a bit distracted, and my marks weren't always the best, often getting only C's and the odd B. Of course, my parents never knew there was anything wrong with my grades until the day I brought my report card home, some 3.5 months into the year. They were often shocked, and a bit upset when they learned that my marks weren't what they expected. They learned, as did I, that more frequent monitoring of my progress was essential to allow for course corrections as needed. They began looking at every test I brought home, and I can still remember practicing my spelling with my mother, while she made us dinner. Staying close to progress is the only way to be sure you reach your intended outcomes.

The reality, however, is that you're busy, and presumably, your team is as well. For that reason, you'll need to set up the weekly meetings I referenced earlier to monitor your team's progression closely.

If you don't, there is a risk that you'll miss steps, and bring the entire machine to a grinding halt.

4. No Measures to Support Monitoring of Progress

Next to insufficient monitoring, having inadequate or incorrect measures is the significant risk to the success of your machine. For example, if you begin introducing aspects of your Funnel of Magnetism but use a success measure of "new sales closed" to monitor its success. There are too many steps between attracting and closing your buyers to use this measure. Considering your funnel is at the beginning of your Unstoppable Sales Machine, a more reasonable measure would be inquiries from buyers who match your ideal buyer profile.

Set the right measure for each area of your machine to ensure you are reviewing the right metrics, allowing you to make course corrections as necessary.

5. Unrealistic Expectations and Timelines

I recall helping an accounting firm introduce their machine, and after three months, the owner asked why their business hadn't doubled. We were only halfway through implementation. It will likely take you between six and eight months to see a significant jump in sales if you have dedicated support to introduce the components of your sales machine, testing and adjusting as you progress.

Yes, I know that's a long time, but I'm not about to mislead you and tell you your sales machine will take a week to launch. That would be ludicrous.

In some instances, implementation can happen, and results come faster because of aspects of the machine already being introduced. I have some clients that have seen bumps in sales within the first five months, so it's possible. I want to ensure you have realistic expectations for how long your machine is fully functioning and driving your sales results.

6. Failing to Assess Risk and Develop Mitigating Plans

When introducing changes and ensuring your sales machine implementation is successful, some risks must be considered. These risks can include:

- Having an insufficient capacity for handling any new business you acquire.
- Accepting new customer accounts that require a significant level of service that restricts your ability to support and oversee all areas of your sales machine.
- Finding new employees to support the expansion and acceleration of your machine.

These are all risks that may occur, on top of the everyday dangers of running and operating a business.

It would be wise to identify all potential risks and prepare some mitigating actions. However, I've always been a fan of a plan for the worst, hope for the best. It's the best way to ensure that nothing throws you off your goals.

7. Inability to Gain Support from Key Employees

Although we spent time in the previous chapter discussing how to get your employees on board with your machine, there is always a chance that a key employee who hasn't read this book may not support your sales machine.

I typically find this is most common with your top sales performer, who, although they won't admit it, sees your Unstoppable Sales Machine as a threat to their reputation and livelihood. However, it doesn't have to be this way. In my experience, giving them a copy of this book, a leadership role in the implementation, and then providing a guarantee of compensation is a great way to engage them.

Be aware, you may need to pull out a few stops when it comes to getting critical employees hired, and if they don't jump on board, you may have to stop the ship and let them off.

8. Insufficient Time and Priority Placed on Implementation

Earlier, we discussed how most strategies fail in their implementation. Success requires adequate time, resources, capacity, and focus. This same risk exists for implementing your sales machine. You will need to dedicate time for yourself and key employees to get your sales machine up and running.

If you treat your machine implementation as a top priority, there will always be time available, which is the only way to ensure a successful implementation.

9. Unwilling or Unable to Remain Nimble during Implementation

To relate this point to a famous parable: If Jack is nimble and Jack is quick, you might want to hire him to help you introduce your machine. All jokes aside, introducing a change of any kind requires flexibility and skill. So, particularly when running your sales machine in parallel to existing practices, make sure that you and your team quickly react to changes, challenges, and opportunities.

STORIES FROM THE SALES FLOOR

A client in the manufacturing sector was implementing their Unstoppable Sales Machine. The CEO contacted me as he was concerned that a potential new client was so big, he wasn't sure they could service them. He was thinking of turning down the business opportunity. Nonsense! We quickly discussed the potential risk areas, identified some mitigating actions, and then pulled together my client's team to discuss with them.

To my client's surprise (not mine), the team was thrilled with the opportunity to land this considerable client and quickly began sharing ideas to overcome the potential hurdles. If you want to capture new customers and get your machine up to speed quickly, you'll have to be agile in how you approach every unique situation.

10. Ineffective or Infrequent Communication throughout Implementation

As you can tell from our discussions so far, the path to success in fully implementing and realizing the success of your Unstoppable Sales Machine is in engaging your team in the process. You do this through communication. Every step I've outlined, every potential pitfall or risk are all things you'll need to share with your team. In doing so, you'll engage them in your vision, which will increase their passion and enthusiasm to see your machine come to life.

HOW FREQUENTLY SHOULD YOU COMMUNICATE?

Well, I've always been a fan of holding morning briefs with your sales team, but weekly at a minimum. Use a simple structure for these meetings such as wins for the week, areas to introduce or improve, and upcoming priorities. If you do this daily, a 10-minute meeting will suffice. However, weekly you will need an hour to cover everything and allow team input and ideas. When introducing your machine quickly and effectively, communication among your team is critical to your success.

Remember that anyone or a combination of these potential issues can derail your machine, so use them as part of your implementation planning to ensure you have the most excellent chance for success. Now let's discuss how to ease your existing buyers and customers into your machine.

So, with your plan for implementation set and under way, let's discuss how to scale and grow your machine (and your sales).

11

Advanced Strategies to Accelerate Your Sales

With your Unstoppable Sales Machine now being launched (you have started to introduce various components, haven't you?), you're likely wondering how you can scale your machine (and your sales) up. After all, one of the benefits of having your Unstoppable Sales Machine is that you can scale up sales as your ability (and desire) to handle more customers increases. In this chapter we'll discuss how to accelerate sales results by scaling up your machine, and methods to slow your sales down (although I'm not sure why you'd ever want to do that!).

TUNING YOUR MACHINE FOR OPTIMUM PERFORMANCE

When I was younger, any trips we took as a family meant that if we wanted to listen to music, we'd need to continuously tweak and adjust the radio dial. No satellite radio in those days! The more you tweaked and adjusted the dial, the clearer the station and sound quality would become. Your Unstoppable Sales Machine is no different. Minor tweaks and adjustments will have a significant impact on the performance of your machine, resulting in faster conversion of customers, larger sales closed, more referrals, and so on.

Let's look at an example.

If you were to visit my website today, at www.shawncasemore.com, you'd find various free resources that will help you accelerate your sales. My site

DOI: 10.4324/9781003252641-15

wasn't always this well laid out, initially only containing a blog and some contact information. However, in recent years, I have added several additional features based on feedback from my buyers who are seeking sales best practices to improve my visitors' experience. You'll recall I referred earlier to creating a buyer feedback loop, which provides you with these kinds of insights.

Here are some examples of features I've added based on buyer feedback:

- A live chat feature to allow visitors to connect with me instantaneously.
- A list of services that describe how I can help visitors accelerate their sales growth.
- Various free tools and resources to help with individual selling performance.
- My Thursday Thrive newsletter, in which I share best practices for selling in today's economy.
- Easy access to my *Sell More with Casemore* podcast.
- The ability to purchase any one of my books.

Quick note. If you'd like to get short, pithy, and practical best practices for selling in today's economy delivered direct to your inbox, just visit www. thursdaythrive.email.

You'll recall from our earlier discussions around the Funnel of Magnetism that a website is only one component of your sales machine. However, considering the amount of time buyers spend researching before they buy, having an up-to-date website and online presence *that is helpful and offers your ideal buyers value,* is imperative.

Until this point, we've discussed where you can find ideas and insights on how to improve the various components of your machine; however, here is a shortlist to get you started:

1. Request feedback from employees involved in various aspects of your machine, including sales, marketing, inside sales, customer service, and so on.
2. Ask for suggestions and ideas from buyers on making their experience better.
3. Solicit recommendations from various partners you'll engage in introducing your machine, such as CRM providers.

4. Capture leads, referrals, and opportunities through involvement with your buyers' associations.

5. Identify opportunities for improvement based on observing your competition.

6. Interview potential buyers and ask what would convince them to invest in your product or service.

When you continually look for ways to solicit and adopt buyer feedback gathered by your sales machine, you'll become agile in your approach to engaging with buyers, which means that regardless of what changes happen with the market, the economy, or in how your buyers prefer to buy, you'll always be able to generate sales. Moreover, continual improvements will serve to shorten buying cycles, speed up conversion, and improve your closing ratios.

Earlier we discussed that it takes at least eight separate touchpoints to move a buyer through a sale. Let's take a moment then to look at all the critical touchpoints you have with your buyers, and how to ensure you remain agile in how you improve both the frequency and value of each point.

TOUCHPOINT OPPORTUNITIES WITH YOUR BUYERS

This is a good time to discuss the various touchpoint opportunities you have with buyers, and how you can use your machine to influence those touchpoints—speeding up your conversion from buyer to customer.

Considering it takes at least eight touchpoints to reach a buyer and today's buyers spend so little of their time with sales, we want to ensure that we add value at every interaction with our buyers. To optimize your machine then, there are several touchpoints you'll need to ensure you add value during, as follows:

1. **Initial Point of Awareness**: The point at which the buyer first becomes aware of your company, products, or services. To satisfy this touchpoint ensure that everywhere your buyer finds your company, its products, or services, there is first a reason for them to connect

with your company (i.e., an offer of value), and second a clear means for them to reach and communicate with you. Use the RUSH value model to identify what you might offer and be sure to offer clear and easy means to reach you.

2. **While the Buyer Is Conducting Research**: While your buyers are researching, they are going to come across your company (if you've introduced your Funnel of Magnetism). When they do, they're likely to visit the following at minimum:

   a. Google (or Bing) to search your company.
   b. Your website (to look closely at what you're offering).
   c. Your social media presence (i.e., LinkedIn, Facebook, etc.) to confirm relevance.

   Considering this, you need to be present and active in any area you can to engage with your buyers. Examples include having a live chat feature on your website, actively monitoring and responding to social media likes and comments, and so on.

3. **When Your Buyer Has Questions (and Wants to Engage)**: These touchpoints are crucial if you are going to integrate your buyers into your machine, so ensure that anyone who may engage with a buyer (e.g., reception who is using questions—qualification hurdles—to direct a call) has a script and recognizes what they can offer that's valuable to your buyer. Using the example of a receptionist, being friendly, ensuring a buyer is directed to a person, not a voice message, and following up with the buyer to ensure they did connect with someone and have their questions answered, are all examples of adding value in this touchpoint.

Since I don't know anything about what your product or service is, I won't digress on further touchpoints that your sales team will need to be on top of, considering this can vary widely depending on your offering, sector, and so on. What I will say is this. Every single time your sales team engages with a buyer, they had better be adding value. Additionally, you should have a mechanism in place to ensure all touchpoints your sales team perform include a follow up.

Lastly, on the topic of touchpoints, just remember that we speed up conversion (and the close) when we add value. Considering all the ways in which buyers may find and engage with your company, how can you add value? If you're unsure, go back and review Chapter 7 again to get some ideas on how to do this.

ENTICE YOUR TEAM TO PERSONALIZE EVERY BUYER EXPERIENCE

It goes without saying that for your Unstoppable Sales Machine to be effective, you'll need to ensure that every touchpoint with a buyer is not only packed with value, but it's also personalized. We've discussed the power of personalization as a key strategy to set yourself apart in today's marketplace.

Aside from recognizing where personalization should exist along your buyer's journey, we need to ensure that in our haste to get your Unstoppable Sales Machine up and running, we never inadvertently lose sight of the value that personalization provides our buyer. Automation and speeding up sales processes are all great, but not if they come at the price of reducing the personalized experience of our buyer.

When introducing automation of any kind, whether you are considering adding auto-email responses or using voice mail for after hours, always be wary of the impact these can have on the buyer's experience. Remember, our goal is to connect with buyers when they are ready and serve them by adding value and being personal. Sometimes automation is not advisable when it may have a negative impact on our buyer's experience.

It's a good time to remind you as well that there is a direct co-relation between responsiveness and personalization. We've talked at length about why and how to ensure you are responsive to any buyer's question, need, or inquiry. However, responsiveness cannot come at the expense of delivering a personalized experience.

A study published by Salesforce suggested that 81% of business buyers say the experience a company provides is as important as its products/services.[22] Our work to date suggests it's even higher than this, driven by the increased complexity of B2B decision-making and a desire to ensure that a solution a buyer considers *meets all the criteria they have identified as necessary.* If this doesn't appear to be the case, the buyer is not likely to engage with sales.

In my book *The Unstoppable Organization*, I shared how companies like Zappos and Southwest Airlines (under Herb Kelleher's leadership) had built and scaled their business on a foundation of providing an exceptional and personalized customer experience. I'd argue that the stakes are even higher when attempting to scale your sales with today's buyers. Giving anything less than a personalized experience is detrimental to your goal of attracting and retaining new customers.

The key message here is that although responsiveness is a critical component of your Unstoppable Sales Machine, personalizing every buyer interaction is still paramount. The more you can personalize every buyer interaction, the faster you'll convert buyers into customers.

Personalization is not as tricky or labor-intensive as you might think but instead simply requires more focus and attention paid to how buyers are engaging (and being engaged with) during their journey. Therefore, when you consider opportunities to improve your responsiveness, always consider if what you are thinking will impact your buyer's experience. If not, move forward, but if there is any doubt, err on the side of caution to ensure experiences remain a focal point of every interaction.

In my experience, there are three reasons why a company doesn't make personalization a priority:

1. Employees don't recognize (and aren't rewarded for) the value of providing an exceptional buying experience.
2. Employees are measured and rewarded for being productive without considering how personalized they make each interaction.
3. Senior leaders prioritize money and profits over their people (not recognizing that reversing how they prioritize can lead to more sales and higher profits).

Instead of falling into this trap, set yourself and your company apart from your competition by testing and ensuring that all buyer contact points are personalized. Here is a checklist to get started:

1. Are your outbound communications (i.e., emails, texts, voice messages) personalized to address the buyer by their first name?
2. Do you respond personally to all inbound contact points such as web forms, phone calls, and emails?

3. Are presentations personalized to include the buyer's name and their company name?
4. Are examples shared and discussed with buyers personalized to be relevant to their company or industry?
5. Are case studies and white papers shared with buyers all personalized to their market or industry?
6. Are testimonials or references personalized to each buyer's industry or sector?
7. Is your sales team trained to ask for and use the buyer's name during every discussion?
8. Is your sales team accustomed to asking for and remembering the names of the buyer's team who are referenced or join in on calls? Do they repeatedly reference those names?
9. Do you have personalized methods to follow up with any buyer who inquires?

With our goal of sustaining a personalized experience for every buyer in mind, let's talk about the language you'll need to ensure you use when interacting with each buyer. After all, in sales language is a tool of the trade, no different than a wrench is to a mechanic.

LANGUAGE TO ACCELERATE THE SALE

Earlier we discussed how to get your entire team engaged in building and supporting your machine. You'll also need to invest some time with your sales team themselves. I'm presuming that your team already knows how to sell, so these are advanced strategies to take their performance to the next level.

When we speak, the questions we ask, our inflection, tone of voice, and volume all serve to drive our buyers' curiosity, interest, and engagement. It's the adage, "it's *not what you say, but how you say it*" at work. Considering the importance of language in the sales process then, focusing on consistently improving the language our sales team uses is critical if we are going to accelerate our sales.

Several years ago, I developed a program to help sales professionals improve their language skills. The program focused on the language we must use in B2B selling to be successful, breaking it down into the most critical components, for example:

- The language you use when you first meet the buyer to drive curiosity.
- The language used to transition a buyer from curious to interested.
- What language to use to move from interested to "give me a quote."
- Language to flush out and rebut objections.
- The language to use to move toward a close.

Although this program is quite popular for sales teams selling B2B, many companies tend to forget just how important language is when it comes to their marketing materials, websites, inside sales scripts, and so on. This is a huge oversight, and one we need to address.

Let's start with the obvious. Language is an essential component to successful selling, whether you decide to sell in-person, online, or a hybrid approach using both.

Russell Brunson, the co-founder of Clickfunnels™ and a global expert in selling products and services online, has been offering a training program to all new users of his company's software called the "One Funnel Away"™ challenge. There are entire modules dedicated to helping users understand the language to use in their landing pages and scripts. Russell recognizes that even if you are selling products or services entirely online using videos, landing page scripts, and email, that language is critical.

The language you use must weave into every touchpoint with your buyer and should meet the following criteria.

Criteria for effective language that speaks to our buyers:

- It speaks to the specific issues, challenges, and opportunities our buyers are facing.
- It's relatable and easy to understand (no difficult words, acronyms, or tech-speak).
- It always highlights the buyer as the focal point, not us, our products, or solutions.
- It reminds the buyer of why they are considering you, your company, and its products or services.

- It ensures the buyer feels like they are not alone, or stupid, or that they made a mistake.
- It includes small nuances that transition the conversation toward conversion.

If you haven't been paying attention to the language your sales team uses or the language on your website or in your sales materials, you might want to take some time to reassess and pay close attention to what you say and how you say it.

Use the following points to validate how effective your language is at speaking to your buyer:

1. Our buyer-facing roles all use scripts that have been crafted to speak to our buyer.
2. Best practices on language that has been successful in converting customers are frequently shared among our sales and marketing teams.
3. Our marketing language aligns with the language that our sales professionals use.
4. We speak using the phrases and terminology of our buyer and their sector, rather than ours.
5. Language we use reassures our buyers they are not alone, and that we can help.

BUILD YOUR UNSTOPPABLE SALES MACHINE

For a printable version of this checklist and other resources designed to help you introduce your own Unstoppable Sales Machine, visit www.unstoppablesalesmachine.com.

If you've ensured that all the language you use meets these criteria, then let's discuss how to crank up your machine for even more sales.

12

Dial-In Your Sales: Scale Up or Slow Down Sales with Your Machine

We've discussed the components of your Unstoppable Sales Machine, how to launch it, and how to get your employees to support your efforts. In this chapter, we'll cover the steps necessary to scale up your sales quickly, as well as how you can slow down your sales when and if circumstances require such.

Although much of what we will focus on is how to scale up your sales, sometimes scaling back is necessary. As we emerge from the pandemic of 2020, for example, many companies have faced challenges obtaining products and services due to supply chain issues. Suppose you are in a situation where you have difficulty finding products, components, or services to provide or even complement your offering. In this case, you can slow down your Unstoppable Sales Machine by simply slowing down the activities at the front end.

The power your Unstoppable Sales machine possesses is that you can adjust the volume of leads and buyers you have by adjusting various activities within each component of your machine. For example, if you're launching a new product, you may decide you want to slow down inbound leads to ensure a successful launch. Alternatively, you may need to raise cash or increase profits, in which case you can quickly ramp up new activities.

With an Unstoppable Sales Machine, you have complete control over the volume and consistency of your buyers and leads.

DOI: 10.4324/9781003252641-16

SCALING UP ATTENTION: THE FOUR SOURCES OF NEW BUSINESS

Many of the business owners and executives I work with want to scale up their sales; at least, that's what they think they want to do. However, something that always sticks with me is something my mother has said since I was young, "be careful what you wish for." Wise words, particularly when it comes to increasing your sales quickly. Scaling up your sales must be done methodically; otherwise, you run the risk of not being able to serve and satisfy your buyers, which can torpedo your machine (and your sales).

While working with a distributor, the President told me that his team would do whatever was necessary to generate new sales. His eagerness was because his sales team did not see results from their current sales activities.

Upon investigation, it became clear that my client's company was, in many ways, a best-kept secret. Sure, they were investing in some activities to attract attention, including posts on social media, content on their blog, and some cold outreach. The reality was, however, unless you knew the owner or landed on their website (which did not rank well in Google, so landing on it was highly unlikely), chances are you would never happen across them if/when you needed their services.

His situation is not all that uncommon. Getting your ideal buyers' attention, the first component of your machine, is the most common contributor to mediocre sales. If you're not widely known, it doesn't matter how good your product or service is; no one will know about it (and it'll be challenging to make a sale). The main objective of the front end of your machine then is to overcome this challenge and amplify (and capitalize on) your presence. We need everyone to know who you are if we are ever going to have an opportunity to convert them into paying customers.

The key to amplifying your presence (and scaling your sales) requires you to focus intently on excelling at four components of your Unstoppable Sales Machine. The more you can improve your activities and execution in each area, the greater your opportunities to sell. Note these are already components of your machine, but the strategies I'll share are advanced, building on the success of your implementation.

The four advanced strategies to scale your sales are as follows:

1. Targeted Outreach

In the previous example, although the CEO had people on his team doing targeted outreach, they offered no value to the buyers when they connected. As a result, the outreach was hurting rather than helping them to generate new business opportunities.

Applying the Unstoppable Sales Machine model to his business, we quickly designed a value-packed presentation to solve their buyers' most significant challenges. Then, using his list of qualified buyers, we relaunched an outreach campaign inviting them to this exclusive event. Finally, the topic included the language based on specific feedback from his ideal buyers relative to what they wanted to learn more about, based on the problem presented.

2. Rocket Fuel Referrals

Although the CEO received the odd referral, they were sporadic and seldom solicited. Considering his company was already well established, they had a long list of thrilled customers. We introduced our Rocket Fuel Referral strategy that regularly connected with three key groups to solicit and obtain referrals.

1. Existing clients
2. Potential clients
3. Past clients

I can still remember when he called me excited a week after introducing our Rocket Fuel Referral process, saying his team had received their first referral after only asking a handful of people. He was almost surprised that it worked. I wasn't.

3. Strategic Partnerships

One of the best avenues to generate new business is aligning your company with those who sell to your ideal buyers but offer something complementary. For example, think of a car dealership that offers a car rental service. So often, these are two distinct businesses, but the synergies and opportunities to partner and share business opportunities are endless when the two are combined.

In my client's situation mentioned previously, we identified and vetted complementary partnerships with other organizations that could offer additional value to his customer base and who, in turn, could introduce their customers to the value his company provided.

Examples included:

- Other software companies selling complementary software.
- Training companies that offer complementary products.
- Associations who supported his ideal buyers.

4. Market Provocation

Like many of his competitors, my client had fallen prey to mimicking his competitors. His website was like theirs; the language on the website was similar, marketing materials were identical, and his processes for generating leads were identical. Everything that he did was the same as his competitors.

To help his company stand out, we introduced market provocation. This strategy involves setting a distinct path in how the market perceives you and your company. For example, as every one of his competitors was playing up the risks associated with cybersecurity (which they could help minimize), my client began discussing how cybersecurity was a minor risk. So, instead, his buyers should invest their IT resources to help grow their business. The key is to pick a provocative approach to stand out in the market, and so long as you can support your claims, it's one of the best ways to get noticed and elevate yourself among your competition.

The most successful companies recognize their weaknesses and explore these four areas, designing a strategy to guide their implementation. Some use my 1-Day Sales V.I.P. for this purpose, while others take a less formal approach.

To help you design your strategy for each of these four areas, use the following questions and solicit input from various stakeholders across your company, including inside sales, outside sales, sales agents, customer service, and so on.

QUESTIONS TO SCALE UP MARKET ATTENTION FOR YOUR COMPANY

1. Do we consistently identify and pursue targeted (ideal) buyers?
2. Is there a process in place to bring these targeted buyers into our Unstoppable Sales Machine?

3. Do we capture lessons learned to improve the effectiveness of our outreach consistently?
4. Is there an expectation of soliciting referrals from all buyers and customers?
5. Do we have a process or system in place to capture these referrals?
6. Do we reward buyers or customers who provide us with referrals?
7. Are best practices on capturing referrals shared widely among our team?
8. Do we frequently identify, assess, and engage with partners who can increase our reach?
9. Is there a win/win/win approach to these relationships we identify?
10. Where it makes sense, do we enter formal agreements with our partners?
11. Does our marketing language provoke our ideal buyers to get them to take notice?
12. Is the language our sales team uses provocative enough?
13. Do we take counter stands to our competitors (and can we back them up)?

If you've perfected your approach in each of these areas, then you'll want to take the next step in scaling up your sales.

SCALING UP YOUR SALES: THREE STEPS TO GENERATING MORE REVENUE

To capitalize on any increased attention and opportunities you generate, you'll need to improve and equally scale up your conversion activities. Rather than replicate or accelerate what you are already doing, start by considering where you can adjust to improve your conversion or closing ratio.

Figure 12.1 shows what can happen to your revenue generation if you don't introduce new and improved strategies and practices.

Here are the three most common areas you'll want to dive into and assess what improvements or changes would have the most significant impact.

FIGURE 12.1
New Sales Opportunities.

1. Sales Skills

When it comes to selling, your Unstoppable Sales Machine and the now scaled-up attention-gathering activities you've introduced will place the pressure squarely on your sales team. For you to avoid losing the opportunities your efforts are currently generating, you'll need to ensure your sales team becomes effective at three things:

1. **Language**: What your sales team says has an enormous impact on your selling ability. As a result, to scale up your sales, you'll need to recognize what language to use to transition the buyer from inquiry to interested and interested to closed.
2. **Dealing with Objections**: The ability to solicit and effectively respond to objections. Although we are only dealing with your ideal buyers, there will still be objections, and the better equipped your sales team is to deal with them, the faster they'll convert.
3. **Follow Up**: More sales result when your sales team becomes good at follow-up. For this reason, you'll want to ensure the entire team is following up in a manner sufficient to engage and then move the buyer (and the opportunity) forward.

Aside from advancing your sales team's skills, there are other areas you'll want to improve upon to scale up your sales.

2. Enabling Technology

Earlier, we discussed the power of enabling technology to ensure your team is spending the predominance of their time on revenue-generating activities. As you engage with more buyers, you'll want to ensure that technology works for you, not against you. Use the following three questions to assess the best use of technology to increase the efficiency of your sales team:

1. Can you automate to improve the productivity of your sales team?
2. Can you use enabling technology to help upskill your sales team?
3. What menial but necessary tasks can you achieve through technology?

As I mentioned earlier, the number of technology options out there that can help you improve the efficiency of your sales process is almost overwhelming. For this reason, you need to lead with these questions to ensure you are pursuing and selecting the right technology that will support your machine.

3. Sales Processes

We've discussed at length the importance of ensuring your sales processes are sufficient to support your team in being consistent and using best practices, but not so overburdened that they stifle creativity. In addition, as you scale up your sales, you must review your processes to minimize any bottlenecks, clarify any areas of confusion, and realign in support of any technology changes you may wish to introduce (following review of the second point just mentioned).

Some questions to consider in assessing the effectiveness of your sales processes are as follows:

1. Where are the most significant bottlenecks or delays in your sales processes?
2. Where are the most frequent mistakes occurring? What might you need to revisit or clarify?

3. What changes in technology may have influenced your sales processes? What updates should you make?
4. What points in your processes should you revisit with your sales team to ensure alignment and understanding?
5. What processes should you convert to video and make easily accessible to your team to support consistency in your sales approach?

Working through these questions while you assess each area will identify the changes and areas for improvement that will support scaling your sales. In my experience, this is not a labor-intensive task, and you can typically complete this in one day (the reason I developed my 1-Day Sales V.I.P.).

SALES SCALE-UP FRAMEWORK

To assist you in scaling up your machine, I've devised a simple framework that you can use. It covers critical components of each of the four scale areas and sales activities.

Figure 12.2 represents my Sales Scale-Up Framework.

FIGURE 12.2
Sales Scale-Up Framework.

To use the framework, ask yourself the following questions, then use the responses to develop focus areas and establish supportive action plans and accountability for their implementation.

1. Are we fully exploiting each area for sales growth? If not, why?
2. What should we stop, start, or keep doing (for the best results)?
3. What can we do to amplify our current success?
4. How will we monitor progress to ensure our changes/improvements are working?
5. Who will be accountable for each area?
6. How frequently will we review our progress?
7. How will we hold ourselves responsible for ongoing success?

Use the responses to these questions to identify:

- 2–4 strategic areas of focus.
- 4–6 key priorities (to be accomplished).
- Measures of success for each priority and each strategic area of focus.
- A champion for each strategic focus area.
- A team to pursue each key priority.
- A communication protocol to keep everyone apprised of progress, challenges, and opportunities.

With some preparation and forethought, you can quickly and easily devise a sales scale-up strategy to use and further capitalize on your Unstoppable Sales Machine.

When I was younger, my wife and I moved around a bit, using each house as a "fixer-upper" to sell and make some money to move on to the next home. I would rush around painting rooms, and generally, they looked okay. Then I would visit my friend Mark, who was also painting various rooms in his house, but his always looked so much better. He and his wife spent time doing color tests on multiple walls to figure out what looked the best; he had figured out a 10mm roller worked best to avoid paint ripples on the wall, and a low gloss paint ensured the walls were washable but not so shiny that every single crack or nail pop appeared. I learned very quickly that you need to slow down to speed up when something is essential.

Don't rush through this step because without fully capitalizing on these four areas, you'll miss out on all the inbound leads and inquiries that you'll need to ramp up your machine fully.

SCALING BACK YOUR SALES (GASP!)

I promised earlier that you could use your machine to slow down sales, so although that's not why most of you are here, it's an important point to touch on.

When it comes to the various activities you'll engage in to gain attention, capture ongoing referrals, and convert new buyers, success results when you find a cadence. That is, you do something enough times that you can expect to see results.

I've written three books now, and although my goal is not to become a number one bestseller, the cadence of writing and releasing a new book every few years is essential if I want to demonstrate thought leadership. I never expected, when I wrote my first or even second book, that "okay, I'm an author now, so I can stop writing." It doesn't work that way.

Neither does your machine. You need to develop a rhythm and cadence in each area of your Unstoppable Sales Machine to experience results. You'll have complete control over increasing the level of activity in each region (which will help you scale up sales) or decreasing the activities in each area (which will have the opposite effect). Fewer requests for referrals, for example, will lead to fewer referrals. It's simple math.

If you want to slow down your machine, look at the front-end components of your machine, and the activities under way, then identify those that have the most significant impact, and scale back your efforts.

Some examples might include:

- If you are gaining the most leads from an association website where you publish content, scale back the content or ask for your profile to be removed.
- If networking at specific events provides you with many leads, participate less often.

- If you gain most of your leads from a strategic partnership, meet with them to discuss ways to scale back leads (without hurting the relationship).

When you slow down activities at the front end of your machine, you'll have fewer conversions and sales. However, strategically, when you want to ramp activities back up, it won't take long to see results.

Lastly, I'd recommend leaving more extended sales cycle activities (like cold outreach) alone; as they take longer to see results, you'll want to leave these in play to avoid taking too long to ramp back up.

Use the following steps (Figure 12.3) to slow down the sales and leads generated by your machine.

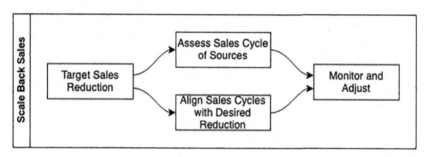

FIGURE 12.3
Slow Down Sales.

FORMULA TO SCALE BACK YOUR SALES

1. Identify the current leads and sales generated by your machine.
2. Identify the reduction you'd like to achieve.
3. Confirm the duration of the reduction period (i.e., three months, six months).
4. Assess the sales cycle of each activity within your sources of new business.
5. Align those with a shorter sales cycle to your reduction period.
6. Adjust input volumes based on current outputs.
7. Monitor closely.
8. Ramp up activities again as you approach the end of the slow-down period.

Now that we've talked about how to slow down the results of your machine let's dive into something a bit more exciting. I call this "domination," and it's what the most successful companies set their sights on when it comes to introducing and fully appreciating their Unstoppable Sales Machine.

Let's get after it!

13

Set Your Sights on Market Domination

For some, scaling up your sales isn't enough. You have ambitions of achieving complete domination of your industry or sector. The good news is that your Unstoppable Sales Machine is the system you'll need to achieve this level of sales success. Before I get ahead of myself, let's first confirm what I mean by Market Domination.

The *Oxford Learner's Dictionary* defines market share as "the amount that a company sells of its products or services compared with other companies selling the same things."[23]

When it comes to selling, the idea of Market Domination is not for everyone, but as William S. Burroughs once said, *"When you stop growing, you start dying."* Although this might seem an extreme perspective to hold when it comes to sales, selling is a numbers game. When you stop working to generate new sales opportunities, they'll quickly dry up.

There are times when pursuing domination of your market might make sense for your company, so let's start here.

WHY PURSUE DOMINATING YOUR MARKET

There are several reasons why the pursuit of increasing your sales to the point of dominating your market will make sense.

- You have a unique product, service, or idea that will revolutionize your market.
- There is a gap in the market that you can satisfy without any competition.

DOI: 10.4324/9781003252641-17

- You are entering a highly competitive sector and need stretch goals to survive.
- Your board, shareholders, or equity partner has expectations of domination.
- Your drive and personality are such that just "making sales" isn't enough.

Keep in mind our earlier discussion about the Laws of Atrophy and that there are always forces pushing against your ability to continue increasing your market share. These pressures typically include competitive, market, customer, workforce, and government pressures. Consistently generating new selling opportunities then is a means to overcome the laws of atrophy, ensuring you avoid complacency and, in turn, don't succumb to any (or all) of these pressures.

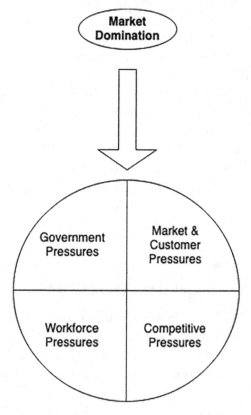

FIGURE 13.1
Dominating to Overcome Pressures.

Whatever your reasoning, market domination is possible if you strategically use your Unstoppable Sales Machine. The reality is, in most markets, there is already sufficient supply to satisfy demand, so if you want to sell more than you are today, you'll need to capture market share from your competitors.

Now, before we dive into how to dominate in your market, let me give you some examples of companies that you'll recognize who have taken this "domination" approach and succeeded . . . so far.

COMPANIES WHO DOMINATE IN THEIR MARKET

When Apple arrived on the scene back in 1976, co-founders Steve Jobs and Steve Wozniak wanted computers to be small enough to fit inside people's homes. Having seen the computer my father first worked on at his job back in the late seventies, I can tell you this was an undertaking. My father's computer at work filled an entire room, and it wasn't small by any shape of the imagination.

Steve Jobs, who carried this vision throughout his time at Apple, used strategies like those discussed in this book to achieve total market domination.

Examples of Apple's Unstoppable Sales Machine in action:

- Apple was clear on who their ideal customers were and ensured their products and features satisfied the needs of these customers.
- Jobs himself interrupted his customer's expectations with his unique product announcement presentations; all dressed in black with no distractions.
- Apple's products brought value to their customers with clean, white packaging that was simple and packed full of features and additional items most of their competitors didn't offer.

Whole Foods is another excellent example of a company that set its sights on dominating its market and has used its very own Unstoppable Sales Machine to support its efforts.

Before it was trendy to eat healthily and protect the environment, Whole Foods was setting the bar and continuously capturing new market share from other long-standing competitors. Whole Foods was ahead of its competition, taking such initiatives as stopping the use of plastic bags, which was launched in 2008, well ahead of the now popular trend.

Example of Whole Foods' Unstoppable Sales Machine in action:

- Since being established in 1980, Whole Foods has remained clear on their ideal customers and recognized that this segment would continue to increase as healthy eating became increasingly popular.
- By banning all artificial colors, flavors, and preservatives while having strict policies about animal welfare in the products they carry, Whole Foods sets itself apart in the market. It adds significant value to customers who seek only the highest quality of grocery products.
- By focusing on customer experience and becoming a destination for friends to gather, Whole Foods adds value to their customer's grocery shopping experience, something that most of their competition doesn't.
- Like Apple, these unique aspects of Whole Foods result in customers becoming raving fans, resulting in a referral machine that has fueled their continued growth and expansion.

Whole Foods dominates and captures market share with more than 430 stores across Canada, the United States, and the U.K.

The last example we'll look at is Ties.com, a leader in selling ties for over 15 years. There likely isn't a more competitive market than ties when you consider that any store selling formal men's (and women's) attire also carries ties.

Examples of how Ties.com have used their Unstoppable Sales Machine include:

- Hyper focusing on their ideal customers, setting themselves apart from men's clothing stores.
- They are interrupting their ideal customers' expectations by providing a convenient and hassle-free experience in shopping for accessories by providing a 100-day no-hassle return policy.
- Use responsiveness as a critical strategy to set themselves apart. Questions posed through chat or forum get a response immediately.

We can glean from these examples of diverse companies in different industries that each company has achieved market domination with an Unstoppable Sales Machine.

When you look beyond the apparent differences in the products and services these companies offer, what you'll find are some standard practices at play (many of which you'll recognize by this point in this book):

1. **They are clear on who their ideal customers are.** You won't find Apple trying to sell whole foods, nor will you find Whole Foods attempting to create and sell a new smartphone. These companies focus on their ideal customers and what they want. Ties.com, for example, started out selling ties of all kinds, and over time has expanded into socks and shirts, all complementary (and necessary) for their ideal customer to accompany their purchase.

2. **They focus intently on doing one thing very well.** For example, Whole Foods has never lost its focus on bringing natural foods to the market, using a supermarket approach. Apple has never turned its back on introducing better technology than its competitors, and Ties.com, well, I'll let you guess what they focus on doing very well.

3. **They add value to their customers.** For example, no one ever believed that they needed an iPod until they experienced one. The idea that you could buy and save only the songs you like, holding them in something as small as a money clip, was genius. The convenience and affordability made the iPod more popular than its predecessors.

4. **They grow through word-of-mouth referrals by their raving fans.** My first laptop when I launched my company back in 2009 was a Lenovo. It worked okay, but as I began to create content such as podcasts and presentations and travel with my iPhone, the inconvenience became frustrating. Several colleagues suggested I try a MacBook and, now on my fourth, I haven't looked back since.

5. **They capitalize on the weaknesses of their competition.** Ties.com recognized that most clothing comes from overseas, resulting in boring designs and few choices. According to Omar Sayyed, the CEO, Ties.com provides superior products ethically made and designed to keep their customers looking good for years to come. If you disagree, they offer a 100-day return policy. Ties.com made its mark by capitalizing on the weaknesses of its competition.

As you can see from these examples, companies that seek domination in their market use their own Unstoppable Sales Machine to do so. The components of your machine are the core ingredients to not only create unstoppable sales for your company but to crush your competition.

DOMINATE YOUR MARKET: PUTTING YOUR MACHINE INTO OVERDRIVE

If dominating in your market is something that interests you (or is necessary), then use the following questions to assess what areas of your machine to focus on to dominate.

1. Is my product or service distinct, or is the market saturated with competitors?
2. In what markets and regions do we have significant sales today?
3. In what markets or regions would we like to generate or increase sales?
4. What are the gaps to capturing new sales (opportunities) in these markets or regions?
5. What components of our machine would support closing these gaps?
6. What additional skills, resources, and technology would support closing these gaps?
7. What is the best starting point for introducing these changes? How long will it take?
8. How will we monitor our progress and the success of our machine components?
9. How often will we meet to assess our progress?
10. Who should champion this growth? Who else should be involved?

You can see that domination requires working through the exact steps we've laid out in this book, applying them to the product or service you want to achieve domination with and in the markets or regions you want to dominate in.

If you already have an Unstoppable Sales Machine in place, this will be simple to do. If you don't, but market domination is your final objective for introducing it, then build it keeping in mind that for each component you introduce, ask yourself if it addresses your most significant gaps to achieving domination. The answer to this question will determine how much time and effort you put into introducing the component.

TAKING THE NEXT STEP: INTRODUCING YOUR VERY OWN UNSTOPPABLE SALES MACHINE

When we began this journey, I shared that if you want to create a consistent and predictable increase in your sales, you need an Unstoppable Sales Machine. Of course, it will take some work on your part, but as you can tell from the examples and case studies shared, the benefits far outweigh the effort.

Here's the key. Today's buyers and how they buy have changed and will continue to change. Selling the old way, like "feet on the street" or "dialing for dollars," can still be effective, but your success rate continues to diminish. Instead, we need to get in front of our buyers' research, empower them to buy, and mine these relationships for more new business.

I can tell you, though, that the benefits of building your machine far outweigh the effort and time you'll put in. Additionally, even if you only develop and introduce a few of the components we've discussed, you'll still see a positive impact on your sales. That's the power of your Unstoppable Sales Machine.

Here's my final question for you. What is the first step you'll take to building your very own Unstoppable Sales Machine?

Let's get after it!

Conclusion

Building and introducing your own Unstoppable Sales Machine isn't simple work. In many instances, it'll require you to re-think and change how your sales team and supporting departments like marketing and customer service work together.

My goal in writing this book was to provide you with a framework that you can introduce into your business to simplify and create greater control over your sales. Treat this book as a guide or playbook that you can refer to as you introduce your Unstoppable Sales Machine.

Now that you've finished the book, you're likely wondering what to do next. I've laid out the book to provide you with the priority order to introduce your Unstoppable Sales Machine. My recommendation would be to return to the first element of your Unstoppable Sales Machine and assess what changes or improvements are necessary. Then, with the first element complete, move to the second, and so forth.

The key will be to get the support of your team to ensure the long-term success of your machine. Don't rush this step! Instead, engage them in the process. When you do, the ideas for improvement will be theirs, resulting in a greater level of acceptance and an increased willingness to accept and adopt the changes.

There will be times when obstacles, delays, or challenges will test your patience. Other times you'll want to skip ahead to experience faster results. When you reach these points, I would suggest that you take a break and spend time revisiting the successes you've had to date.

My personal goal is to help as many executives, leaders, and sales professionals accelerate their sales as possible. After all, selling is a noble profession, and without it, business as we know it wouldn't exist.

To help you with your journey, I've developed several resources you can access for free. First, you can visit unstoppablesalesmachine.com to print the many templates, checklists, and vast array of other resources I've created to complement this book.

You can also visit my website at shawncasemore.com, where I publish a weekly blog, video, newsletter, and podcasts.

Committed to Helping You Accelerate Your Sales,

Shawn Casemore

References

1. An, Mimi. 2019. "Global Buying Behavior in 2020 [New Data]." *Hubspot.* https://blog.hubspot.com/marketing/buyer-behavior-statistics
2. Marketo. 2017. "Which Digital Channels B2B Buyers Use to Engage with Vendors." *Marketing Channels.* September 1. www.marketingcharts.com/customer-centric/customer-engagement-79971
3. Sharpe, Rachel and Weber Shandwick. 2019. "Tork Survey Reveals Loss of Lunch Breaks Weighs Heavily on Millennials." *Essity.* June 4. www.prnewswire.com/news-releases/tork-survey-reveals-loss-of-lunch-breaks-weighs-heavily-on-millennials-300860283.html
4. Sophy, Joshua. 2017. "62 Percent of Small Businesses Owners Say Facebook Ads Miss Their Targets, Weebly Reports." *Small Business Trends.* January 3. https://smallbiztrends.com/2017/01/do-facebook-ads-work.html
5. Wagner, R. Polk and Thomas Jeitschko. 2017. "Why Amazon's '1-Click' Ordering Was a Game Changer." *Wharton Business Daily.* September 14. https://knowledge.wharton.upenn.edu/article/amazons-1-click-goes-off-patent/
6. Bagnes-Amat, Arnau, Liz Harrison, Dennis Spillecke and Jennifer Stanley. 2020. "These Eight Charts Show How COVID-19 Has Changed B2B Sales Forever." *McKinsey & Company.* October 14. www.mckinsey.com/business-functions/marketing-and-sales/our-insights/these-eight-charts-show-how-covid-19-has-changed-b2b-sales-forever
7. "New B2B Buying Journey & Its Implication for Sales: The B2B Buying Process Has Changed, Has Your Sales Strategy?" *Gartner, Inc.* 2019. www.gartner.com/en/sales/insights/b2b-buying-journey
8. McSpadden, Kevin. 2015. "You Now Have a Shorter Attention Span Than a Goldfish." *Time.* May 14. https://time.com/3858309/attention-spans-goldfish/
9. "How Sales and Marketing Intelligence Drive Improved Business Outcomes." *ZoomInfo.* www.zoominfo.com/resources/how-sales-marketing-intelligence-drive-improved-business-outcomes
10. Hattar, Marie. 2021. "Five Digital Strategies for Improving the B2B Buying Experience." *Forbes.* May 17. www.forbes.com/sites/forbescommunicationscouncil/2021/05/17/five-digital-strategies-for-improving-the-b2b-buying-experience/?sh=5039638c4717
11. Caplow, Beth. 2021. "Three Seismic Shifts in Buying Behavior from Forrester's 2021 B2B Buying Study." *Forrester.* April 14. https://go.forrester.com/blogs/three-seismic-shifts-in-buying-behavior-from-forresters-2021-b2b-buying-survey/
12. Branham, Leigh. 2013. "The 7 Hidden Reasons Employees Leave." *Leadership beyond Limits.* June. https://leadershipbeyondlimits.com/wp-content/uploads/2013/06/WhyPeopleLeave-Branham.pdf
13. Wikipedia. 2011. "Moneyball: The Art of Winning an Unfair Game." *Columbia Pictures.* https://en.wikipedia.org/wiki/Moneyball_(film)
14. McSpadden, Kevin. 2015. "You Now Have a Shorter Attention Span Than a Goldfish." *Time.* May 14. https://time.com/3858309/attention-spans-goldfish/

15. Merriam-Webster. *Definition of Value.* www.merriam-webster.com/dictionary/value
16. Zetlin, Minda. 2019. "Blockbuster Could Have Bought Netflix for $50 Million, But the CEO Thought It Was a Joke." *Inc Magazine.* September 20. www.inc.com/minda-zetlin/netflix-blockbuster-meeting-marc-randolph-reed-hastings-john-antioco.html
17. Wikipedia. "Howard Schultz." https://en.wikipedia.org/wiki/Howard_Schultz
18. Klein, Christopher. 2019. "How McDonalds Beat Its Early Competition and Became an Icon of Fast Food." *History.* August 7. www.history.com/news/how-mcdonalds-became-fast-food-giant
19. "New B2B Buying Journey & Its Implication for Sales: The B2B Buying Process Has Changed, Has Your Sales Strategy?" *Gartner, Inc.* 2019. www.gartner.com/en/sales/insights/b2b-buying-journey
20. Toman, Nicholas, Brent Adamson and Cristina Gomez. 2017. "The New Sales Imperative: B2B Purchasing Has become Too Complicated: You Need to Make It Easy for Your Customers to Buy." *Harvard Business Review.* March–April. https://hbr.org/2017/03/the-new-sales-imperative
21. Carucci, Ron. 2017. "Executives Fail to Execute Strategy Because They're Too Internally Focused." *Harvard Business Review.* November 13. https://hbr.org/2017/11/executives-fail-to-execute-strategy-because-theyre-too-internally-focused
22. Hou, Zontee. 2018. "8 Key Statistics from Salesforce's State of the Connected Customer Report." *Convince & Convert.* www.convinceandconvert.com/research/state-of-the-connected-customer-report/
23. Oxford Learner's Dictionaries. *Definition of Market Share.* www.oxfordlearnersdictionaries.com/definition/english/market-sharej

Index

Printed in the United States
by Baker & Taylor Publisher Services